CASSELL STUDIES IN PASTORAL CARE AND PERSONAL AND
SOCIAL EDUCATION

COUNSELLING IN SCHOOLS

11/98

Other books in this series:

R. Best (editor): *Education, Spirituality and the Whole Child*

R. Best, P. Lang, C. Lodge and C. Watkins (editors): *Pastoral Care and Personal-Social Education: Entitlement and Provision*

G. Haydon: *Teaching about Values: A New Approach*

P. Lang, R. Best and A. Lichtenberg (editors): *Caring for Children: International Perspectives on Pastoral Care and PSE*

P. Lang, Y. Katz and I. Menezes (editors): *Affective Education: A Comparative View*

O. Leaman: *Death and Loss: Compassionate Approaches in the Classroom*

J. McGuiness: *Counselling in Schools: New Perspectives*

J. McGuiness: *Teachers, Pupils and Behaviour: A Managerial Approach*

L. O'Connor, D. O'Connor and Rachel Best (editors): *Drugs: Partnerships for Policy, Prevention and Education*

S. Power: *The Pastoral and the Academic: Conflict and Contradiction in the Curriculum*

J. Ungoed-Thomas: *Vision of a School: The Good School in the Good Society*

P. Whitaker: *Managing to Learn: Aspects of Reflective and Experiential Learning in Schools*

CASSELL STUDIES IN PASTORAL CARE AND PERSONAL AND SOCIAL EDUCATION

Counselling in Schools
New Perspectives

John McGuiness

CASSELL

London and New York

Cassell
Wellington House
125 Strand
London WC2R 0BB

370 Lexington Avenue
New York, NY 10017-6550

First published 1998

British Library Cataloguing-in-Publication Data

A catalogue record for this book is available from the British Library.

ISBN 0-304-33354-9 (hardback)
     0-304-33356-5 (paperback)

Library of Congress Cataloging-in-Publication Data

McGuiness, John.
    Counselling in schools: new perspectives/John McGuiness.
    p.   cm. – (Cassell studies in pastoral care and personal and social education)
    Includes bibliographical references and index.
    ISBN 0-304-33354-9 (hardcover). — ISBN 0-304-33356-5 (pbk.)
    1. Educational counseling – Great Britain.   I. Title.   II. Series.
LB1027.5.M367   1997
371.4 – dc21
                                                      97-2324
                                                        CIP

Typeset by The Midlands Book Typesetting Company, Loughborough
Printed and bound in Great Britain by Biddles Ltd, Guildford & King's Lynn

Contents

Series editors' foreword

John McGuiness wrote the first book to be published in this series back in 1993. Entitled *Teachers, Pupils and Behaviour: A Managerial Approach*, it set the tone for the series as a whole, exemplifying the level of professional relevance and quality of argument which we hoped for in the series. We have awaited the sequel with keen anticipation, and we have not been disappointed.

This is an excellent book and one which could not have come at a more important time. After a decade or more of domination of schooling by a regime of imposed curricula, assessment and inspection, the pendulum has begun to swing back towards the recognition that there is much more to education than this. Spiritual, moral, social and cultural development have emerged as rediscovered priorities, and there are signs that the slide into the 'culture of exclusion' may have been stemmed. Perhaps the day when schools again begin to appoint specialist counsellors (as they did in the 1970s) is not far off, but some important changes in perception and understanding need to happen first.

Consider the following true events:

A student in a comprehensive school dies of meningitis. Many of his classmates are traumatized and the school as a whole is plunged into an unprecedented period of grief and adjustment. His form tutor – in only her third year after qualifying – finds herself coping with his tearful, withdrawn and frightened peers, taking their distress upon herself. She does a wonderful job from intuition and natural empathy, but this is not enough. She needs training in the skills to counsel them, and she needs counselling to help her cope.

An injudicious disclosure of a piece of personal information by a student teacher leads to suspicion of child abuse. An over-zealous head and her deputies interrogate every child in the class, generating a contagious hysteria. They call this process 'counselling', and use the hysteria as proof of the need to do it. No firm evidence of abuse is found, but many of the children would benefit from real counselling in the aftermath.

A youth retrieving a football from a garden next to his school falls through a greenhouse and bleeds to death. The school and community are shocked and stunned. The local authority draws on its child guidance and social work staff to assist, which they do, and with good effect. But the media reports of the 'bussing-in of teams of counsellors' create a distorted image which builds on stock prejudices against the 'do-gooders' of the caring professions.

As these examples show, the potential for counselling in educational settings is enormous, but so, too, is the lack of training for counsellor roles and the scale of misunderstanding about counselling itself. Those who counsel seem to be in no-win situation: either they are expected to have the answers to all known problems (and are criticized when they don't), or they are ridiculed as pseudo-professionals who need their own heads examined. In the school context, their plight is exacerbated by those who are only too ready to argue that what kids need is not an 'agony aunt' but personal fortitude and some old-fashioned discipline.

John McGuiness's book takes the reader well beyond the part which counselling skills might play in the repertoire of teachers' classroom strategies to an exploration of what counselling itself really is. It is both an introduction to the theory of counselling and a practical training source with useful exercises and provocative questions. Above all, it is a very powerful case for the value of counsellors in schools. It is a case which we hope will receive careful consideration from teachers everywhere.

Ron Best and Peter Lang

Introduction: new perspectives

It seems arrogant for an author to claim that he will offer 'new perspectives'. Ecclesiastes, and many others, tell us that there are none: 'nothing is new under the sun'. When the subtitle was suggested to me, my reaction was that in a sense, I ought to be biblical, cut my losses and accept that it had all been said. What, on reflection, stopped me doing that was a double realization: first that though counselling has a large and growing literature, it is not a static entity, but an activity in the process of becoming. It has changed since the pioneer Rogers challenged the orthodoxies of his own psychodynamic training in the late 1930s and early 1940s, laying the foundations for a new, psychotherapeutic, client-centred approach. It has changed, too, since British pioneers like Daws and Hamblin developed training courses for teachers in the 1960s, fundamentally as part of a prophylactic approach to mental health, and it is still changing as the Bests, the Langs, the Ribbinses of the current scene offer new critiques, new visions, indeed new perspectives, on what it is to be a teacher, asking us to be proactive in responding to the full developmental range of our pupils. Pastoral care and personal and social education require all teachers to have basic counselling skills, and some teachers to have specialist expertise in counselling, beyond the basic.

The second part of my double realization was a growing awareness by me on in-service education and training (INSET) courses that increasing numbers of teachers were indeed moving considerably beyond 'basic counselling skills' – counsellors and 'teachers-who-counsel' were beginning to reappear in our schools. I knew, too, that this was occurring in a context in which there was little written *specifically* on counselling *per se* for teachers. In this text I try to focus on counselling itself, rather than as an adjunct, a peripheral, to teaching. What *is* counselling, where has it come from, does it work, do we have time for it, is it really different from what good teachers have always done, is it an appropriately educational activity?

I have tried, therefore, to do two things in this text: first, to argue that our pupils have an entitlement to the highest-level counselling skills that we, as classroom teachers with basic counselling skills or as specialist counsellors, can offer; and second, to get inside the activity of counselling itself, beyond the basic skills, deeper than the initial, basic responses we make to pupils in difficulty –

not to argue that operation at this level is an obligation on all teachers, but to indicate clearly the roots from which the basic skills we all try to offer have grown. Counselling as an activity which runs parallel to and beyond the traditional activity of the teacher merits serious attention in its own right.

The first, brief chapter places personal values high on the agenda, with a suggestion that they are a potent, and sometimes unexamined, influence on our practice. What are my views on the nature of the child, of human beings; how do I view the purpose of education and so on? I offer it not to convert, but to invite fellow professionals to accept the important influence of their values on their practice, and to perform a careful scrutiny of the values that drive their own activity as teachers. The second chapter tries to argue that the provision of counselling services, from both a generalist and a specialist point of view, is under pressure in the utilitarian climate of current government policies towards education, and that in addition to this being ethically unacceptable, it is also indefensible, even in terms of the utilitarian agenda set us by the government. Industry and commerce are offered as two areas where the company accountants accept the value of counselling services in organizations. The third chapter moves from a global, organizational justification of counselling to a consideration of it from the professional and therefore ethical point of view of the person working with children in classrooms. It analyses in greater depth the nature of counselling, offering a 'map of the territory' on which it is possible to locate all human helping interactions. It argues, too, that the very nature of teaching takes us into the realm of socio-emotional helping, and that consequently we need skills beyond the academic/intellectual to discharge fully (professionally) our responsibilities. Chapter 4 takes a further step forward. Given that all of us in the classroom need basic counselling skills, what precisely lies beyond those skills? What is counselling? The one constant feature of all our lives is change. As teachers we work every day with young people who with varying commitment pursue academic change, while in the midst of all the social, emotional, moral, physical, sexual, domestic and vocational change that we call adolescence. Thus the chapter offers a detailed analysis of counselling perceived as a relationship, a process and a range of skills and techniques. Brief, illustrative vignettes attempt to put flesh on the structure.

Having identified the key characteristics of counselling, in Chapter 5 I move into a clear distinction between the skills and duties of the classroom teacher-counsellor and the specialist counsellor. How can we make sure that pupils can find help when they want it? Issues of responsiveness to pupils, 'first aid', referral, support and the problem of re-entry for pupils who have been absent or referred outside the school are discussed. Chapter 6 looks in detail at the taxing challenge for the counsellor of working with deep material. Most teachers will not counsel at this depth, but I do see it as beneficial for us all to have an awareness of the existence of these deeper levels, which are a persistent influence on our work in the classroom. We may not work with this material as counsellors, but this material will impinge on our work in the classroom. When teachers on INSET courses express reservations about counselling, it is usually an anxiety about the nature of deep material and how best to respond to it. The bereaved, the abused and those suffering post-traumatic stress are already in our classrooms; this chapter suggests that we can do more than timidly avert our gaze from them. Counsellors will be familiar with the themes of Chapters 7 and 8: all the help we try to give our clients is part of a process that allows the client to change, in the direction desired by the client. Thus the two chapters look at facilitating decision-making and action planning by the client. Chapter 9 examines current thinking on a range of key pupil challenges facing all teachers.

Finally, in Chapter 10, ourselves. Counsellors, according to the various ethical codes currently governing the profession, are required to have regular 'supervision'. That is, for every five or six hours of counselling they are expected to have an hour of supervision. This consists of an opportunity to discuss cases currently being worked on, in a professional and confidential analysis with a qualified supervisor. It provides the important facility for the counsellor of permitting a sharing, an updating, an objective, supportive critique of progress and a chance to examine unresolved personal difficulties that may be awakened by specific cases. Supervision is a recognition of the fact that to look after clients properly, we need to attend also to our own personal and professional needs. While teaching in Chicago in the early 1970s, I experienced the teaching equivalent of supervision. Each of us on the staff was expected to sit in on, and on a different occasion be observed teaching by, a colleague, with whom we then had a professional, and sometimes personal, discussion on our teaching. I found it exhilarating and a little scary. Professionally it was one of the most stimulating types of professional development I have ever experienced. This chapter looks at the issue of the teacher/counsellor's own mental health.

At the end of each chapter, a number of exploratory or skill development exercises are offered on the grounds that the important thing about counselling is to do it. While many of them can be done without colleagues, peer feedback and sharing is an invaluable resource. Thus the exercises will be most beneficial if done with a good group facilitator, in the company of trusted colleagues.

For Jack and Emily,
who taught me so much about caring for young people

CHAPTER 1

Nothing up my sleeve: counsellor values

This opening statement (following an example set in many of Carl Rogers's publications) is an attempt to say to the reader, 'This is me, this is where I am coming from, these are my values and they infuse what I write and how I teach.' It is an attempt to be 'congruent' in a Rogerian sense, and is also an invitation to readers to engage in a similar search for the values that underpin their own practice. Given Gilmore's model of counselling (1980), which claims a central influence on practice of a counsellor's personal philosophy, it seems appropriate and honest to set out my ethical stall in this way at the outset.

I set out to write this book acutely aware of the contribution of the pioneers in school counselling, particularly Peter Daws and Douglas Hamblin, whose giant contributions make me hesitate in this endeavour. The only possible justification is that schools, and the society in which they operate, have changed so radically since 1988 that it seems opportune not to write a critique of their work, but to look with fresh eyes at the impact of the education reforms on the 'mental health enhancement' ideals set in motion by Daws and Hamblin. Daws, citing strong historical evidence, concluded a paper in 1967 thus: 'The country that does not care for its young destroys its future. Since mediaeval times, Europe has been affronted by England's indifference to, neglect of and brutality towards its children.'

I am convinced that when the history of Britain in the last quarter of the twentieth century is written, commentators will light on the dehumanization of education as a cultural change that had enormously damaging effects. That is not a statement of criticism against any political group; it is quite simply as close as I am likely to get, as a professional in education, to apologizing to the children, including my own, who have lived through the shambles. I warm to Morrell's (1989) analysis that the values that produced the 1988 Education Act were 'a fusion of Hayek's vision of individual freedom . . . Friedman's monetarist economic thesis and . . . the Conservative acceptance of a hierarchically structured society'. The Act moved us away from a vision of education that honoured social responsibility and saw schools and children as too precious to be subjected to the unpredictable rough-and-tumble of the market-place. Instead, it reinforced the hierarchical lore crystallized in the nineteenth-century hymn, which praises the stability of a society that left unchallenged 'the rich man in his castle, the poor man at his gate' – a manifesto for cardboard cities the world over.

At a recent research seminar in my university, I listened to the then Minister for Schools defending the government's education policy. He emphasized the twin engines by which the policy was, he said, being driven – choice and diversity. During the question-and-answer period that followed his presentation, I asked whether he had forgotten a third, and to me much more influential, engine – the market-place. Was it not central to government policy that education should be subjected to the 'discipline of the market place'? He agreed that was indeed the case and re-emphasized that the choice and diversity his government wanted to provide would flow from that very discipline.

I needed to pursue that deceptively benign scenario. That very same day I had been engaged in INSET at a good primary school in a very deprived inner-city area. The headteacher had introduced me to, let's call her 'Debbie', a 7-year-old whose physical development suggested she was a few years younger. The head asked her, 'What did you have for your breakfast this morning, Debs?' The child, without a moment's thought or embarrassment, replied, 'nothin', Miss'. It was 10.30 a.m., and this child had not yet eaten. 'What did you have for your supper last night, love?' Puzzled look – a new word, supper. Try again. 'What did you have to eat before you went to bed?' 'I had my dinner [i.e. school lunch] here with youse.' Her last meal had been at noon the previous day, in school. Meanwhile, less than ten miles away, the children at a city technology college were being welcomed with cooked breakfasts. Was this, I asked the minister, the market place in operation? Had we decided that Debbie merited only limited investment? Was not a major characteristic of the market place that there were winners and losers? What did current government policy offer the losers? His answer chilled and depressed me: 'You are an educator. You must not confuse your role with that of a social worker.'

Will Hutton (1994a), while accepting that the market place is efficient at generating wealth and stimulating change, speaks of a 'psychological black hole at the heart of capitalism'. Its logic is to treat relationships as commodities that are bought and sold, and in the process have their value destroyed. Many of my colleagues working at all levels of the education endeavour, from universities up to primary schools, struggle in this black hole, trying to maintain relationships as something more subtle and reliable than a 'commodity'. We have perhaps previously taken for granted the notion that the focus of the teacher's work must be persons. This must now be argued for and restored to its position as the driving force of education.

At the heart of my ethical position, as both a teacher and a counselling psychologist, is the stance that the concept of 'loser', central to a market-place philosophy, is alien to education and counselling, and that when it is used as a construct in educational debate, the educational endeavour is irretrievably mutilated. One of my hopes in writing this book is that it will contribute towards the 'rehumanizing' of education.

There are, of course, many approaches to counselling, underpinned by different psychological theories. This text focuses powerfully on the Rogerian, humanistic approach, not to devalue psychodynamic or behavioural approaches, but as a recognition of the consistent evidence (Rogers, 1951; Truax and Carkhuff, 1967; Carkhuff and Berenson, 1977) that the *person* of the counsellor is the key therapeutic factor. This is probably best summed up by Norcross and Guy (1989), who warn counsellors not to be seduced by the 'myth of disembodied treatment' or overwhelmed by 'the tyranny of technique'. This is not to say that behavioural techniques do not have uses in school or that the depth work of psychodynamic therapists and therapists who work with metaphor and imagery is not a rich source of help to children; it is simply to choose the baseline on which all therapy plants its feet – the establishment of a relationship which is in itself therapeutic. The teacher who uses counselling skills will communicate that enhancing relationship to the pupil/client; the counsellor-teacher or the specialist counsellor may well develop a wider repertoire of skills and techniques, but must be ever-mindful that the evidence shows clearly that the prerequisite for their effectiveness is the quality of the relationship he or she is able to create with the client. Looking at key writers in the influential field of behavioural psychotherapy, I certainly agree with Krumboltz and Thoresen (1976) that 'most client problems are so complicated that no single technique proves sufficient'. I note too the assertion in their 1969 text that behavioural therapy works most effectively within a safe relationship: 'in this beginning stage', they say, 'the listening, reflecting and clarifying of feelings are essentially those procedures that have been advocated by Carl Rogers and others' (p. 52). While it is probably not provable that we can 'love people better', *any* techniques, according to the research cited above, deployed within a loving, respecting relationship will produce therapeutic effects. Rogers is both historically and psychologically the starting point for the counsellor.

As I get longer in the professional tooth, despite the fact that I use the *techniques* of gestalt, behavioural psychology, imagery and group dynamics, I find myself looking increasingly at the Rogerian focus on the person of the counsellor and the relationship he or she establishes with the client. In helping our pupils to live more confident, competent, self- and other-respecting lives, what we *do* in the therapeutic relationship is less influential than who we *are*. Speaking of children with special needs, Gilliland and McGuiness (1989) produced a diagram that suggests how the Rogerian emphasis has significance for the non-specialist counsellor, the teacher using the skills of the counsellor in the classroom (see Figure 1.1).

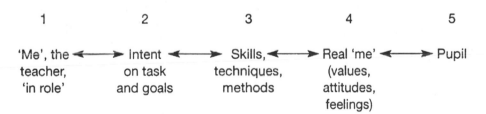

1	2	3	4	5
'Me', the teacher, 'in role'	Intent on task and goals	Skills, techniques, methods	Real 'me' (values, attitudes, feelings)	Pupil

Figure 1.1 Mediating influences between pupils and teachers

The suggestion is that element 4 is frequently unexamined, yet influential, in the classroom. In counselling terms, the evidence is that the 'me', the person of the counsellor, is a key variable in terms of therapeutic effect; hence the centrality given to Rogers's work. Using Figure 1.1 as an analytical tool, we can scrutinize, for example, how a teacher (1), wanting to help pupils (5) engage in participatory learning strategies (3), would operate if the teacher were subconsciously but profoundly authoritarian (4). Or in work with an epileptic pupil (5), after a course in first-aid skills (3), how would a teacher (1) cope if he or she were fearful (4) of convulsions? The examples could be multiplied, but the basic point is that 'the real me', unexamined, can too often vitiate good intentions and high skill levels.

So who is this book for? Is it for the specialist counsellor or the highly skilled teacher who has developed and deploys counselling skills as part of a broad perception of professional responsibility? I would hope that it offers insights to both readerships, and to senior managers and governors in schools who have to make decisions on how best to ensure that pupil entitlement to the provision of counselling expertise is met. The arguments that I assemble in the following pages, drawn from the nature of education, from psychology, from the nature of the society within which our young people are growing up, from the hard-nosed practice of the commercial world, leave me in no doubt that schools *ought* to allocate a proportion of their staffing establishment to the provision of counselling for staff and pupils. Clearly, how this is done needs to be set into the context within which the school operates, the nature of its staffing and the availability of expertise in the staff. My own view is that full-time, specialist counselling expertise needs to be available, either in school or at least in a well-monitored referral system. In the current climate, a full-time counsellor as part of the staffing establishment may not be a possibility, and I think the excellent work of McLaughlin *et al.* (1996) offers very practical guidance in using staff expertise within the school's normal staffing as an alternative response.

Exercises

All practical work in counsellor training must be fully voluntary; pressure on the group to participate, intrusion by the trainer, some form of obligation, runs totally counter to the Rogerian acceptance of the wisdom of the client in deciding where to go, how fast and in what direction. Thus, trainers frequently introduce sessions by saying that 'Everyone must feel free to decline to participate in any exercise. There will be no pressure or black looks. This is part of the safety that we would like to be a central feature of the group, and that safety is essential. Can I also say that in addition to safety, groups, if they are to move forward, need generosity in sharing, when that feels comfortable. But you the group will decide your own pace.' The exercises are written in a form that presumes a group of ten or twelve, but they can be adapted for smaller or larger groups.

Safety and challenge

To grow professionally involves more than the intellect, and to operate at a level deeper than the intellect we need to feel safe enough to take the risks all explorers take. The unknown, even quite close to home, can be challenging. The following exercise tries to facilitate a level of disclosure which feels safe and remains comfortable to the individual, but which permits a sharing at greater depth than normal.

Each member of the group is asked to write anonymously on a sheet of paper 'The fears and anxieties I have in this group are . . .' Then the twelve participants share their sheets with the other group members (all mixed up and handed out by the trainer) in a way that preserves anonymity and ensures that each person finishes up with a paper other than his or her own. In turn, the participants then read out the paper they have, as if it is their own, trying to own the feelings disclosed by the anonymous writer, by enlarging on the original statement of anxiety. Thus, I might have received a paper that said, 'I fear that I will not be able to cope with counsellor training from a personal point of view' or 'I always feel stressed in new groups' or 'I am a bit uneasy because I don't know what is going to happen. If it were a science/modern languages INSET I would feel more confident.' The reader of the sheet is invited simply to react to the paper, positively and personally.

Given that the initial invitation is to share feelings, the group is already disclosing at a level that goes deeper than conventional conversation. The attempt to own the disclosure of another person takes each of us into levels of acceptance and empathy which enhance the cohesion and safety of the group. This group, we hope, will become a place in which it is safe to share. Then a second, similar, exercise draws our attention to the potential the group has for developing the participants in some way they desire.

Each group member is asked to write anonymously on a sheet of paper 'The things I hope this group will help me achieve.' Thus twelve statements of aspiration are pooled, then redistributed, so that as far as is possible no one gets his or her original back. Then each person reads someone else's 'hopes' as if they were his or her own, empathizing, getting in touch with another person. The range of twelve perspectives can be challenging, consoling, encouraging. Thus, I may receive from a fellow group member the statement, 'I want to learn more about the theory of counselling' or 'I want to feel more confident in responding to my pupils' problems' or 'I would like to be able to know myself better.' My task is as above: to read it aloud to the group, and in some way to accept any of it that touches my own experience. 'Yes, I hadn't thought of that – I tend to concentrate on the intellectual bit on courses; I would like to know myself better; maybe that should be in the anxiety section.'

There is no formula: each group goes at its own pace and raises its own issues. These two simple exercises are ice-breakers and permit a group to test the safety of sharing feelings. Concepts like acceptance, empathy and warmth begin to appear; relationships go centre stage. When they are completed, the trainer will often draw the exercise to a close by inviting a discussion of reactions to the exercise: has the group climate changed, is it possible to identify how it has changed and what facilitated that change? Perhaps a 'round' will be used in which everyone is invited in turn (anyone can pass!) to complete a phrase like 'one thing that surprised/excited/comforted me in the exercise was . . .' It is important in using rounds to emphasize that the individual inputs are to be simply 'heard', not discussed, analysed, evaluated. Thus, group climate is clearly presented, and the group members know their perceptions are accepted.

Values and the professional

In the final analysis, our decisions are value-based, not logic-based. The role of logic in decision-making and problem-solving is to generate options and possibilities, which can be derived from the data available: 'Given this scenario there are *n* possible courses of action.' The selection of the action to be taken is on the basis of some process of evaluation of the possibilities – beyond the possible, feasible, to the desirable, preferred. Gelatt (1962) established a strong theoretical base for this stance, and it is now widely accepted in theories of decision-making. A consequence of that analysis is the need to scrutinize our values as part of our professional development. The purpose of the exercises is not to establish an orthodoxy, it is rather to permit exploration, so that influential elements in our professional lives can be declared, owned or changed. For a much more detailed treatment of values and their influence in the classroom, see Frankl (1964), Rokeach (1968) and Simon (1978).

Value continuum: this invites participants to place themselves on an imaginary line (this can be a physical line like a row of chairs), according to the value they place on a polarized incident, as follows.

> *Many people argue about materialism, property, honesty and so on – values. Sometimes we declare values that we do not live. For example, I value good health, but for me to live that value, the bottle of malt whisky in my cabinet ought to last longer. Smokers will have a similar conflict between declared and lived values. What about property? Imagine a 1 to 10 scale in which 1 represents a position that says, 'under no circumstances would I ever steal' and 10 would represent, 'if I was certain I would not be caught, and I knew the victim would not lose out in any way, I would take something that was not mine'. Select the number that best represents your position. Am I a '1', a '10' or somewhere in between? Is it easy to be honest, in a group, about my values; and does this hint at counselling challenges? Discuss the exercise, both as a process and as an insight into your values.*

We have been looking at a personal, ethical principle. There I am – I chose 3, not too sure I would resist any temptation, but committed to an idea of honesty and property rights. I may be surprised by others' 'liberal' approach, with their 7s and 8s. No matter; we are not here to judge, but to accept and explore. Now, let's try to put the principle into a practical context.

> *It is three in the morning. You are returning from a long trip, and as you walk through the deserted town centre, you notice that a cash dispenser is rolling out ten-pound notes at a slow but regular rate, one every thirty seconds. There is already a small pile of about twenty on the pavement. You are absolutely certain that there is no camera, that you are not observed. Try to 'be' in that scenario: Christmas approaching; a big phone bill has just arrived; a desperate need for new tyres, road fund licence. Now, the ten chairs in front of you represent a continuum:*

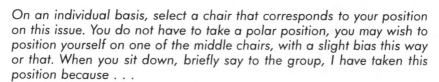

Under no circumstances
would I take the money

Certain that I was
not observed, I would
keep the money

On an individual basis, select a chair that corresponds to your position on this issue. You do not have to take a polar position, you may wish to position yourself on one of the middle chairs, with a slight bias this way or that. When you sit down, briefly say to the group, I have taken this position because . . .

There is no right answer. The purpose is not to establish some form of 'morally acceptable behaviour', but to explore values, to understand that theory and practice sometimes diverge, and that consensus on values is not always present. Can I accept that my values may not be the same as other people's? Do I want to impose mine on them? Using this technique, we can explore attitudes towards authority, the individual versus the community, sexual values, educational values – all part of the initial task set for counsellors by Egan (1986). We first need to come to terms with the 'problematic' in the self. Who am I, really?

A trusted person

In a final exercise, the trainer needs to prepare a piece of stiff card, about two feet by three in area, cut into twelve pieces like a jigsaw. It is important to mark the side of the piece to be written on, so that when the puzzle is made, all the writing faces upwards! In addition, the group will need a piece of backing paper slightly larger than the jigsaw, Blu-Tack and felt-tips.

People are each given a piece of the puzzle, and invited to write on it (right side up) the qualities of one person in their life in whom they have great trust, with whom they feel they can be themselves. Each person does this individually. The jigsaw is then assembled by sticking the pieces with Blu-Tack on to the backing sheet, thus offering a composite view of the qualities of the person who wins our trust. A discussion of the result is led by the trainer, who may want to invite the group to create a prioritized list or simply explore the elements. The final part of the exercise is to invite group members to choose one characteristic they would like to work on enhancing in their training.

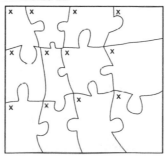

CHAPTER 2

A national curriculum and the rights of pupils

If I had to choose an alternative core concept to 'winners and losers' as a navigational star in education, I would have to travel far to find anything that represented my position better than the following comment from Pablo Casals to Golda Meir, when the cellist was performing the oratorio *El Pesebre* in Israel in 1969.

'Every second we live', he said, 'is a new and unique moment of the universe, a moment that never was before and will never be again. And what do we teach our children at school? We teach them that two and two make four and that Paris is the capital of France. We should say to each of them, "Do you know what you are? You are a marvel. You are unique. In the millions of years that have passed, there has never been another child like you."'

No suggestion of losers there. An almost startling reverence for humanity, yes – and a challenge to me as an educator to divine and nurture that pervasive uniqueness. Yet sadly – and the minister's comments cited in Chapter 1 are merely one example of the dehumanizing philosophy that infuses so much current government policy – I find an almost total absence of the profound respect for persons, expressed so eloquently by Casals, in the piles of documents disgorged on to an exhausted teaching force by the statutory and regulatory bodies which administer the delivery of the National Curriculum in England and Wales. Despite the Dearing Report (1994), and the welcome change seen in its respectful and collaborative tone, schools are still some distance away from a philosophy that puts the uniqueness of the child at the centre of its activity. As a society we have moved away from the vision of the inviolable dignity of the human being to something much colder and more utilitarian. We do not, notably, 'reverence humanity', yet we express surprise when our children kill and torture each other.

In 1979, Her Majesty's Inspectorate published a report (DES, 1979) in which they described 'the personal development of children' as 'the central purpose of education'. Less than two decades later, testing, vocationalism, central control and, of course, the market place have given instrumentality centre stage – people as tools and objects, relationships as commodities. We have had Darwin placed in the classroom, the survival of the fittest, and have created a criminally negligent waste of talent; there is a *rhetoric* of choice and diversity, but the Debbies of this world and their parents will see little of it. Education takes place in an ugly, dog-eat-dog climate; we cannot be surprised that we are creating an ugly, dog-eat-dog society. Dissent (this chapter?) is marginalized as the self-protective knee jerk of the 'educational establishment', while the ideologically respectable gain educational influence which breathtakingly exceeds their competence, experience and vision, and the Inspectorate, which proposed a different, more child-centred agenda, has been destroyed.

The Nigerian Nobel Laureate and university lecturer Wole Soyinka (1972) gives a harrowing account of a series of torture sessions he was subjected to as a suspected political activist during his country's civil war. He describes how, barbaric though the physical pain was, he found it unutterably more unbearable to realize that among his tormentors, beyond the blindfold, were some of his former students. 'What kind of an education', he challenges us, 'allows someone to become a torturer?' That is the kind of cosmic question that stops me in my tracks, as I contemplate the spiralling figures for crimes of cruelty in our society; it is a *human* question and a question for teachers. It raises the issue of the kind of values that drive educational provision. Soyinka's challenge reminds me to face the fact that fifteen thousand hours in my care still leaves some pupils to emerge to batter babies, beat wives, terrorize the elderly and maim each other. What kind of an education *does* allow that to happen? What contribution might the skills of counselling make to increasing the levels of dignity with which people in our schools are treated? Of course, I do not propose to suggest that education bears a sole responsibility here; but I do propose that the question merits serious consideration.

There is no doubt that over the past fifteen years we have seen a major shift at government level in what is perceived as the purpose of education. Our pupils and students are now viewed more as future contributors to the national economy, valuable for that potential contribution, rather than as intrinsically valuable for their humanity. An education system which does not celebrate the value of people for their common humanity is one which edges us closer, with its instrumental view of human beings, to the nightmare described by Soyinka. Said thus, this offers no more than a statement of my personal ethic. I would like to press on to argue that when governments, with a utilitarian view of education, set teachers a limited (SAT-filtered) educational agenda, and measure their success by that agenda, we are in danger of being pushed into a falsely dichotomous view which sets the pupils' and students' human value into some kind of opposition to their ability to contribute to society. My position is that it is not necessary to devalue a pupil's capacity 'to do' or 'to contribute' when we celebrate her or his capacity 'to be'. On the contrary, there is overwhelming psychological evidence (Burns, 1979, 1982; Rogers, 1983) that by concentrating on the unique dignity of the learner, by infusing our teaching activity with genuine respect for the learner, we actually enhance her or his ability 'to do' and 'to contribute'. Unfortunately, there is already some anecdotal evidence that teachers at all levels (my own work is currently in a university) are being driven by a utilitarian education policy to pursue limited, short-term goals which, although they meet the doubtfully valid testing programmes and performance indicators of government ministers, narrow the concept of education and betray the students taught in this way. Hutton (1994b), speaking of markets, catches a flavour of our market-driven schools. He is speaking as an economist of markets, but you may want to try the analysis on what is happening in the new, 'market-disciplined' school. 'They are anonymous. They foster lack of commitment by both parties; they actively promote the restless search for the highest return in the immediate future; they are impatient of failure and setbacks.'

For me, then, a key question to probe the National Curriculum initially is an ethical one: what fundamental perception of human beings does it embody? Does it see them as having intrinsic value or merely consequential value? Do people have only a value consequent on their contribution, or are all our pupils seen as having an inviolable core of dignity that transcends the winner–loser mentality of the market place? And to what extent do the rhetoric and the reality coincide?

I find comfort in the vast corpus of psychological evidence that my ethical position has an empirical support. There is evidence that human beings perform tasks more competently, will learn more effectively, when they perceive themselves as possessed of inviolable dignity and worthy of unconditional respect. One suspects that Soyinka's torturers had little experience of such a climate. Thus, a fundamental task of the teacher is to be able to create a climate of this kind, not merely because of a personal, ethical position, but also because it permits the learner to pursue the academic objectives of the National Curriculum more successfully. The ability to create this climate is a central prerequisite for effective counselling (Truax and Carkhuff, 1967; Brammer and Shostrum, 1982; Norcross and Grencavage, 1989), and is also increasingly seen to underpin effective teaching. Rogers (1983) applies his clinical experience in counselling to the classroom, arguing that a teaching relationship infused by the relationship skills of counselling permits deeper, more comprehensive and better-retained learning.

Rogers offers his readers a reflection of Einstein, that 'it is nothing short of a miracle that the modern method of instruction has not entirely strangled the holy curiosity of inquiry; for this delicate little plant, aside from stimulation, stands mainly in need of freedom; without this it goes to wrack and ruin without fail'. He goes on to identify a number of aims, related to the creation of this facilitative climate, that I find useful as a checklist for a personal 'examination of conscience'. How does my teaching measure up to Rogers's list?

- Does my classroom have a climate of trust; is it a *safe* place for my pupils/students to be; can they take risks or are they fearful and self-protective?
- Do my pupils/students participate in making decisions; do they experience responsibility and its consequences, or are they depowered, driven and controlled?
- Is my classroom a place in which pupils' self-esteem is safe; or do they feel they are not regarded as worthy of respect and courtesy?
- Do I provide the excitement that exists in intellectual and academic discovery; or is my content sterile, regurgitative and narrow?
- Am I comfortable with the classroom's potential for the excitement that exists in emotional exploration and discovery; or do I keep everyone at arm's length, sharing with them a facade behind which I hide?
- Do I communicate to my pupils the notion that learning is a lifelong, enhancing activity; or can they not wait to escape the drudgery of the classroom?
- Do I grow as a person in my school; or am I pinched, limited, only flowering in other environments?

- Am I aware that 'who I am' has greater significance that 'what I do', and that averting my gaze from the former will reduce the impact of the latter?

As I re-read Rogers, I realized how radically the educational reforms since 1988 had changed the focus of our thinking – the Rogerian questions jar, seem out of tune with the time, lack the clarities (or rigidities) of the new testing ethos. In this uncomfortable situation, it seems important and professional to lean on a final recommendation of Rogers: that teachers should base their work on available research, not whim, ideology, political dogma or prevailing fashion.

The theoretical constructs normally offered to the teacher to explain how children learn are drawn from the cognitive psychology of such researchers as Piaget (1926, 1952), Piaget and Inhelder (1958), Bruner et al. (1956), Vigotsky (1964) and Donaldson (1982). What I have to say in no way detracts from their formidable contribution to our understanding of the way that children learn; I would like to argue that from the point of view of many teachers, their research starts too far into the process. The constructs that the cognitive psychologists offer, while they are useful in explaining successful learning, are not so helpful in explaining failure to learn. This, I wish to argue, is because they do not consider in detail the issue of motivation to learn. Instead they move swiftly into the mechanics of cognitive functioning, and that works only when the learners are motivated. Failure to learn seems frequently to be a motivational problem, not an intellectual one, and the analysis of such failures takes us more appropriately into social and counselling psychology than into cognitive psychology.

Piaget certainly regarded learning as in some sense a 'risk-reducing' strategy. The learner, in Piagetian terms, seeks to diminish the disequilibrium brought about when she or he is presented with new, unmastered experiences. The motivation to mastery is the desire to restore order to a disordered personal universe, to re-establish a sense of personal control. But the concept of 'moderate novelty' (i.e. that new experiences need to be sufficiently close to the existing schema of the learner to permit the learner to reach out to the new material) suggests that that includes an element of risk-taking by the learner as well. Gross novelty, though Piaget does not say this, is too risky to pursue, so the learner averts her or his (psychological) gaze from it. If the leap in embracing the new learning is too great, the learner will play safe and stay where he or she is. In this sense, Piaget offers us a clear door into the concepts of 'risk' and 'safety' as key elements in the process of learning.

The American Vera Heisler (1961) offers us a different insight into learning failure, going more boldly through the door half-opened by Piaget. She suggests that the development of mental health is the result of an interaction between two fundamental human tendencies: the need for homeostasis (i.e. a comfortable balance between inner needs and outer forces) and the need for 'differentiation' (i.e. the need we have to grow, develop our capacities, seek stimulation). She sees effective development or learning as a kind of progressive response to challenge, a response which occurs only when the learner has the support of a significant degree of basic equilibrium. Thus, healthy development and learning in the classroom will occur only when there exists a dynamic balance between the learning stimulus and a resilient, basal personality equilibrium which can cope with the ongoing challenge of new material. Both Heisler and Blocher

(1974) argue that children who lack the basic security to ensure tolerable levels of homeostasis will put all their energies into establishing such levels. There will be little residual energy to direct at learning new material and seeking to respond to new experiences. Quite simply, learners who do not feel safe will direct all their energies towards feeling safe, and in a real sense the effective teacher must be an expert at creating areas of safety, the homeostatic state, which will encourage pupils to take the risks involved in learning. In being thrust into a crude pursuit of positions in league tables, in concentrating on the delivery of the content of the National Curriculum, teachers may have their attention diverted from the possibility that their pupils can feel simply too unsafe to reach out to the carefully prepared academic material. Nor is this to devalue that material; it is to draw our attention to the psychological priority of other teacher skills. It reminds us of those occasions when we can teach our socks off, and find that very little consequent learning has occurred in our pupils – and it suggests an explanation of why this might happen.

An explanation for the tendency in some learners to reject the invitation to learn can be found in the work of the self-theorists, like Snygg and Combs (1959) and Burns (1982), or the psychotherapist Rogers (1983). Building on the foundational work of Mead (1934), Snygg and Combs feel able to make this challenging statement: 'the single most important motivator of all human behaviour is the establishment, the maintenance and the enhancement of self esteem'. So important is this need for a strong sense of personal worth seen to be by the self-theorists that they regard its protection as a psychological demand that takes precedence over, for example, the need to take part in academic activity. Lawrence (1973) argued convincingly that a major block to first steps in reading is not intellectual but self-esteem related. He demonstrated that the reading age of children exposed to 'esteem-enhancement' activities, instead of traditional, remediation responses, increased to a significantly greater degree than that of those children who received only the remediation responses. It appears that once liberated from the fear of risk to self-esteem, children were better able to reach out to the challenge of reading. Perhaps we need to ask ourselves in the classroom how many of our reluctant learners are not presenting cognitive or intellectual difficulties but rather are saying to us, 'I'm very sorry, but I cannot address the material you are offering me at the moment. I have a much more pressing need to establish myself as a being of intrinsic value.' Perhaps our pupils are more astute at establishing the priorities of the classroom than we are.

Unfortunately, such psychological evidence has been dismissed as worthless by influential government advisers in the past ten years. Education policy is ideologically driven and thus the presentation of counter-indications to 'reform' is dismissed by an ideologically acceptable but grossly inexperienced elite as irrelevant. Thinking, analysis and critique by teachers were not on the agenda of the advisers of the Conservative governments. Lawlor (1990), attacking the theoretical dimensions of teacher training courses, certainly embraces the Rollo May adage that theory without practice is sterile, but what are we to make of this influential government adviser who objects because student teachers are not taught to teach in a 'traditional' way? Is there any scrutiny of the implicit theories that lie beneath her proposals? She objects that at Durham University (one of several universities she decides to attack), tutors 'encourage students to question issues and to be independent and flexible in response to incidents'. She prefers that departments 'hand down in a didactic manner the received wisdom of the teaching profession'. Perhaps she could at least consider the continuation of the May adage: though theory without practice is sterile, practice without theory is blind and dangerous. The Centre for Policy Studies, which published the paper in question, says that Lawlor's writing was published because it showed 'independence of thought and cogency of argument'. Well, the independence of thought is certainly there; as for cogency of argument, I find it difficult to take seriously a writer who so misunderstands the complexity of teaching that she sees it as the equivalent of acting, playing the piano, driving or swimming! But take her seriously we must, for much of the current orthodoxy being thrust into schools and institutions of education derives from her and her colleagues.

If only Lawlor had paid more attention to a document published two years earlier. The Cadbury Report (1988), seeking to establish stronger links between business and education, asks among other things that pupils in school should develop the skills to have 'sensitivity to the needs and points of view of others; the ability to listen, to question and debate, to support colleagues, to contribute as a member of a team'. The report is not, of course, setting the National Curriculum content on one side – indeed, it sees it as essential. It is, however, rejecting the simplistic views of Lawlor that subject expertise is all that a teacher requires; beyond that subject expertise, she says, 'the skills of teaching . . . can be acquired *only* [my emphasis] through experience, trial and error and careful individual supervision . . . colleges and institutions of education should cease to have anything to do *at all* [my emphasis] with the training of teachers'.

Our students merit much more than the workhouse crusts that the Lawlor vision of education offers. The interpersonal and life skills, the ability to communicate, to cope with change and to work in groups highlighted as essential outcomes of education by the CBI in the report cited above are not peripheral, self-indulgent insertions into the curriculum – they are central to the formation of the effective, confident and competent workforce the country clearly needs. There is an ethical position, a view of human beings, that suggests the desirability of a person-centred approach to teaching; there is, further, a body of psychological evidence that supports the position that this person-centredness enhances pupil performance. Yet further, even in terms of the discipline of the market place, hard-nosed, financially disciplined business organizations are buying, from university schools of education, training in the very skills that are being removed from teacher training. The businessmen see clearly what government education advisers are blind to: that the quality of task performance (the Attainment Targets of the National Curriculum) is enhanced *or diminished* by the teacher's (or manager's) ability (or inability) to offer a 'relationship whose characteristics create for the client, an environment of such safety, respect, and support that (s)he finds it possible to take the risks involved in independence and a creative response to life's challenges' (McGuiness, 1989). It brings us back to Debbie. Put simply, to facilitate the risk-taking involved in all learning, we teachers need counselling skills. McGuiness (1992, 1993c) details how commercial and industrial organizations have a deep and increasing awareness of the distinction between task leadership skills and social leadership skills, and the need for managers to develop both. This a theme which will be examined in the next chapter, since teachers can be seen, in the best sense, as 'managers' of children's learning. If a manager at ICI or Marks and Spencer needs that twin leadership focus to facilitate employee effectiveness, do our pupils in school merit less from us as teachers? More on that later.

Every invitation to learn is an invitation to change. It is an invitation to leave the familiar, the mastered, the comfortable and the position of competence we currently have and to move to a new place, where for a time we will feel unfamiliar, not in control, uncomfortable and incompetent. Every teacher, from the reception class teacher to the PhD supervisor, presents new vistas and experiences to learners, and invites them to become voluntarily incompetent for a while. This is worth reflecting on because it lies at the heart of teaching. Every learner, from Debbie to an employee facing new technology, faces the unknown with varying degrees of trepidation. This, too, is worth reflecting on since it lies at the heart of learning. Under what circumstances would I, or the reader, or Sheila Lawlor, or Debbie, make ourselves voluntarily incompetent, uncomfortable or not in control? For my part, it would only be in the presence of someone who made me feel very safe and very valued. To be able to do that is to develop 'social leadership skills', to attain highly sophisticated teaching skills, to be able to deploy with confidence the skills of the counsellor (Rogers, 1983).

The ability to make someone feel safe is a precious talent. It involves the ability to liberate the recipient from fundamental concerns about self-esteem and personal worth, so that other challenges can be addressed. I suspect I am not alone as we approach the year 2000 in not feeling very safe – we live in a climate of rapid change, where 'being economical with the truth' and being 'one of us' have become the moral watchwords of our society, leaving many of us ill at ease, wondering what the *real* truth is and left out of the decision-making process because we are not 'one of them'. Being in the dark and powerless does not produce a climate in which any of us can feel safe. Perhaps being a teacher as we head towards the millennium involves us in switching on some lights and giving our pupils a sense of power, and the responsibility that goes with power.

Acknowledgement

This chapter is substantially based on a paper which originally appeared in the *British Journal of Guidance and Counselling* (1993b, **21**, 1). The author gratefully acknowledges the publisher's permission to use it here.

Exercises

This chapter has argued the psychological priority of self-esteem as a key element in motivation, industry and achievement. Where it does not exist, our central motivational tendency is to direct our industry to achieving it, thus diverting ourselves from any other activities. The following exercises attempt to get us inside the concept and to use the concept in a personal exploration.

My self

If, as many theorists argue, the most important factor in counselling is the 'self' of the counsellor, a careful analysis of that self seems appropriate. Burns (1979) writes in detail on the structure of the self, suggesting that it is a complex, dynamic reality, which relates the way we perceive ourselves to the ideals we have about 'the good person'. Thus, I lay my self-concept against the values I carry around with me, measuring the extent to which I manage to live up to those values. If I find a huge gap between my perceived self and my ideal self, I am left without 'self-esteem', which is a prerequisite for mental health. It is useful to bear in mind that the socially derived self, i.e. the messages others give us about ourselves, means that we can have different 'selves' in different situations: school, club, home, church, etc. Much counselling has to do with pervasive low self-esteem in clients.

> *Invite the group to imagine that a fairy godmother has agreed to give them five new or improved personal qualities. What interpersonal qualities would you really like to have? Ask them to write the list down individually. Examples might be 'to improve my temper', 'to be less sexist', 'to be more open to children', 'to show off less', 'to be more honest'. Such a list suggests that the writer fails to find a satisfactory match between his vision of his 'self' and some ideal to which he aspires. That becomes material for growth on a counsellor training course.*
>
> *There may be someone in the group who sees himself or herself as in no need of fairy godmother gifts! In this case a more challenging exercise involves asking the group to get into pairs. Each person is asked to list five gifts of interpersonal qualities they would like to give the colleague. 'The gifts I would like to give Tom/Mary are . . .' This adds a socially generated dimension to our self-perception (which itself is very influenced by what others communicate to us about our selves).*
>
> *Finally, a third possibility is to invite the members of the group to produce lists of as many blocks to their interpersonal ability as they can generate. 'What most gets in the way of my relating to other people?' To finish positively, a list is then produced of 'what bits of me enhance my ability to relate to those with whom I live and work'. Again, a social dimension can be added by inviting colleagues in pairs to complete the phrase, 'What I really appreciate about you is . . .'*

In addition to the generation of material and the exploration of self that occurs, post-exercise discussion often generates very insightful material on the issue of the self.

What did they teach you at school?

Classrooms and schools are complex places, in which pupils spend 15,000 hours of the first part of their lives. In addition to formal learning, we all learn things that were not on the curriculum: to be a victim in the playground, to flirt with the right teacher, to be assertive, that I am useless at maths, that girls can shine in science, that some of the best chefs are men, that I have dignity, that I merit respect, that I owe respect – the list is endless. In addition, I may on reflection think, 'I wish I had learned X at school.' Those elements too might be listed: 'to dance', 'to like myself', 'to communicate', 'to know more about sex', 'to be able to change a nappy', 'to be open', 'to debate', 'to cooperate' and so on. Search and be creative.

> *In small groups of three or four, brainstorm onto a flip-chart (i.e. everything goes on, no censoring, analysing; if someone says it, record it) two columns: things I learned at school and wish I had not; and things I did not learn at school and wish I had. It may be helpful to categorize both lists into feelings/attitudes/values, skills/techniques or academic things.*

A discussion of the charts might explore the brief of education. Do we influence the 'self perception' of our pupils? Is our influence considered, positive in effect? Are teachers expected to take too much responsibility? Should we not withdraw from the social, the emotional, the value dimensions of pupils' development? Is it psychologically possible to do so? If not, what is available to us to respond effectively to the enormous challenge we are given? How ought we to distribute responsibility for the task?

CHAPTER 3

Ethical teaching

When Carl Rogers (1983) begins his influential text on the counselling skills needed by teachers with the comment from Einstein cited in the previous chapter on the need to develop in our pupils 'the holy curiosity of inquiry', he is, appropriately, light years away from the narrow, 'didactic' approach and 'handing down of received wisdom' advocated by Lawlor. I find a certain reassurance in being close to Einstein and distant from Lawlor.

Rogers goes on to identify a number of key objectives if we are to engage in the kind of teaching that nurtures curiosity of inquiry, or, in the current vocabulary, education for enterprise. Teachers must, he says, create a climate of trust in their schools and classrooms, encourage students to participate in decision-making, enhance the self-esteem of pupils, create excitement in intellectual and emotional discovery, establish an attitude that learning is a lifelong affair, use research findings to infuse their teaching, grow personally and help students to realize that 'the good life' lies within each of us, not outside of us. That implies personal responsibility and the opportunity to exercise it.

Over a dozen years ago I tried to argue the importance of developing intellectual and emotional openness in pupils: it seemed almost a truism to say that education should open the mind (McGuiness, 1983), yet I find de Bono (1990) still lamenting the impact of 'rock logic' on our perception, creativity and problem-solving abilities – that tendency towards dichotomy, black/white, 'I'm right, you're wrong' thinking. He proposes (and is supported in his thesis by three men who each won the Nobel Prize for physics, and who accepted the invitation to write a preface for his book) a subtler, more sensitive paradigm that will not lock us into the patterns of thinking that have served us previously. It is not a soft option; it is the challenging option of creativity and risk. When I read the detail of the National Curriculum, even with its Dearing review, and the current (1996) proposals to reintroduce selection in schools, I smell rock logic – the rigid patterns of thinking that have served us previously. The engines of our educational endeavour, at least at national level, are driven by inadequate fuel, and we are reaping the results of its fatal flaw: the dehumanizing emphasis on 'task', with little real thought being given to the human beings in the system, and the consequent selfish, fearful society we have created.

I want to argue the case for Daws's (1967) statement that 'mental health is every teacher's business', that the skills of the counsellor are not an optional extra for the teacher, but a fundamental and necessary part of the skills of the effective professional. The teacher who presents himself or herself in the classroom without these skills is lacking in an ability which will *inevitably* vitiate the learning of the students. This sounds extreme, but it has at least a prima facie validity in the extensive recognition in commercial organizations of the need for these skills among their managers (Egan, 1993; Cooper and Cartwright, 1994) and, closer to home, in the unequivocal recommendation 43 of the Elton Report that all new teachers should be trained in the 'basic skills of counselling'. Not to have these skills takes us to the edge of unethical activity – we enter our classrooms under-prepared. For me, a modern linguist, not to be aware of the social and emotional consequences of my teaching places me in the same position as the general practitioner who prescribes medication without awareness of the side effects. It is no more acceptable for me to push that responsibility into the pastoral care system than it is for a rheumatologist to say, 'Take these pills for your arthritis', then, as an afterthought, 'they may damage your liver, but that's not my area. We do have an excellent liver unit [pastoral care system] in the hospital [school].' The basis of my argument is the existence of extensive evidence (Snygg and Combs, 1959; Heisler, 1961; Rogers, 1983; McGuiness, 1993b) that task performance by human beings is influenced for good or ill by the presence or absence in the teacher (manager, change agent) of a number of socio-emotional skills and the ability to communicate certain clear messages to people about their dignity and value.

That said, it is important to define precisely what the terms we are using mean. I am certainly *not* saying that all teachers need to be counsellors. The problem for our discussion is that the word 'counselling' has been used with such a variety of meanings that achieving clarity in the discussion will not be possible until we agree a vocabulary. Perhaps we can best start by looking at descriptive material first, before we move on to a precise definition. When the the King's Cross tube fire, the Lockerbie air disaster, the Zeebrugge ferry sinking or the IRA bomb attack in the City of London occurred, counsellors were made available to the victims; we have an idea that a form of specialist help was involved in helping victims and helpers to cope with the trauma of being involved in such catastrophes. Perhaps we find ourselves admiring the work these counsellors do, and at the same time reflecting that we would find such work very challenging. Or we can recall pupils who, we learn, have been sexually abused, and who are receiving long-term help to overcome the destructive effects of that ultimate developmental insult. Again, admiring those who work in depth with such children, we may find ourselves withdrawing in horror from such pain, grateful that others will offer the help needed. It may help us to view such activity as being at one end of a continuum, the other end of which is something akin to the comments in a DES publication that became a myth in its own time, that counselling involves simply 'having big ears and nodding at the right time' (DES, 1987). We have this gut feeling that large ears and synchronized nodding would have done little, if anything, for the traumatized people mentioned above. It might even have harmed them. But most of us will also have had experiences which lie somewhere between those two poles: perhaps we have come across a crying child in the playground, and after gentle probing discovered that his granny had died at the weekend; or suffered an unusual and aggressive response from a pupil in class, and instead of blasting the young person out of her seat, we have had a hunch that there was some agenda running things of which we had no idea, and responded in a more muted way, looking for ways of helping as well as setting out clear rules on courtesy. We simply tried to be 'there' – supportive, unsure of how precisely to help, but pretty sure that a non-judgemental, warm presence would help. We, in those situations, are using basic counselling skills.

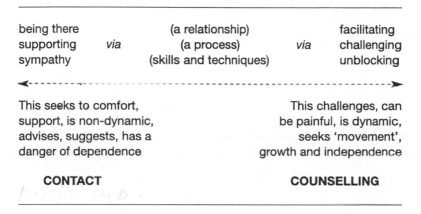

being there		(a relationship)		facilitating
supporting	*via*	(a process)	*via*	challenging
sympathy		(skills and techniques)		unblocking

This seeks to comfort,	This challenges, can
support, is non-dynamic,	be painful, is dynamic,
advises, suggests, has a	seeks 'movement',
danger of dependence	growth and independence

| **CONTACT** | **COUNSELLING** |

Figure 3.1 Human interactions that help: from a continuum from simple contact to counselling

The two end points are set deliberately on a continuum, to emphasize that all human beings when they seek to help each other do so by deploying their interpersonal skills (see Figure 3.1). The difference is a qualitative one, and it merits a very careful analysis. While I would object to the mystification of counselling, the presentation of it as some magic, charismatic, quasi-religious gift that some of us have and others do not, it does seem important to emphasize that, like teaching, it is a skilled activity that requires training and has real potential for harm if practised by the unskilled and untrained (Truax and Carkhuff, 1967; Carkhuff and Berenson, 1977; Egan, 1986). When Eysenck (1953) presented evidence that, in a large sample of neurotic patients, those receiving counselling or psychotherapy had no greater chance of recovery than the untreated group, he seemed to deal a devastating blow to counselling. Only the later work of Truax and Carkhuff was able to show that within the treated group there were variations from therapist to therapist in their success rates. Some therapists had success rates that exceeded the 'spontaneous recovery' rates of the untreated group by 50 per cent – cause for some optimism about the efficacy of counselling. However, given the accuracy of the global figures initially produced by Eysenck, Truax and Carkhuff's disaggregation of the averages indicated that while some counsellors did indeed have positive effects on clients, others actually reduced the likelihood of recovery below the spontaneous remission rate. They went on to produce the seminal training text, *Towards Effective Counselling and Psychotherapy*, in which they identified the consistent characteristics of the effective practitioners. Nor is that to devalue the crucial 'first aid' that occurs on the left-hand side of the continuum. On the contrary, it sees that activity as an important first contact and initial deployment of basic counselling skills. Those of us who work there (with the lad whose gran had died or the girl who is inexplicably and atypically rude) can provide an important holding role until, if necessary, something more detailed can be offered. Moreover, such is the strength of what Rogers (1951) sees as our 'self-therapeutic capacity' that the simple, non-judgemental contact may be sufficient for the client to emerge from that particular challenge without any further help. The basic counselling skills of every teacher may prove sufficient to help students cope with a particular challenge in some cases. The foregoing, then, gets us to the first and key definitional characteristic of counselling: *it is a helping relationship*.

In preparing recently a paper for 70 finance directors from major companies in Spain on the role of counselling in the management of change in large organizations, I was intrigued to discover that there was no word for counselling in Spanish – it led me to a careful attempt to get hold of the specifying characteristics of the word. 'Psicoterapia' was suggested, but I felt uncomfortable with the medicalized feel that that had, despite a tendency in the literature to use the two synonymously. 'Consejo', advice, got the push immediately, because of the 'expert role' given to the advice-giver, and 'asesoriamento', appraisal, failed to catch the subtle complexity of counselling and had overtones of judgement. I settled for 'el counselling', on the grounds that a new word was needed to present a new concept. I was not being awkward, a linguistic pedant, I simply wanted to clear from the minds of my audience false trails offered by the overtones of psychotherapy, advice and appraisal. At the heart of the concept for me is the idea of empowerment. When Carl Rogers in the late 1930s and then in his revolutionary 1942 text *Counselling and Psychotherapy* argued the benefits of taking responsibility for recovery away from the therapist and returning it to the client, he was making an enormously optimistic and respectful statement about human beings. His phrases 'the wisdom of the client' and 'the self-therapeutic capacity' of persons led away from concepts of experts and their ability to tell us who we are and what we might become, towards a more challenging yet still supportive interaction with those who confront challenge in their lives. So, we can add to our definitional ground-clearing a second key element. Counselling seeks to empower the client by *putting the client in charge of the process*.

Rogers shifted responsibility for change away from the expert to the person who wanted to change, bringing us to a fundamental element of counselling: that any change, be it socio-emotional, developmental, matrimonial, taking charge of my life, enhancing my talent, will happen more quickly, with less pain and trauma, with greater possibility of success, when the person who seeks the change is at the heart of and in charge of the process. The implications of this for the classroom teacher, for me as a language teacher, are clear: unless I am willing to involve 'the wisdom of my students' and their 'self-enhancing capacity' in my classroom activity, then the exhausting experience of their resistance and sabotage will be mine. To do so, however, involves that same respectful and optimistic leap of faith that Rogers made, and the development of at least the fundamental interpersonal skills needed to create the kind of environment in which that might occur. To engage in this facilitative teaching is not to convert the teacher into a counsellor, it is to ask from the teacher the basic facilitative skills of the counsellor. The justification for this paralleling of counselling and teaching is that both activities are concerned with change, growth and development. The theme is explored in detail in Rogers's (1983) application of the conditions for effective counselling to the classroom environment, and in a courageous account by Brandes (1981) of her attempt to use Rogerian approaches in the classroom in a challenging inner-city school in the north of England.

In my classroom I seek to help pupils to change; indeed, if they did not change, and for the better, I would expect someone to ask questions about the ethics of my accepting a salary. The useful concept of 'added value' has been damaged by the market-place ambience in which it was first used, but it can, stripped of its ideological baggage, remind us that as teachers we are agents of change. Egan (1993) comments thus: 'change, whether individual or institutional, is messy, emotional, social, political and cultural or counter-cultural in nature. These realities need to be factored into the change process from the very beginning' (p.105). He is talking to senior managers in the world of commerce, but a central part of my argument is that our pupils merit no less support and challenge than their parents in the workplace. How, then, do we 'factor in' the realities Egan identifies as infusing the change process? He is aware that change involves us in leaving the familiar, the well learned, the mastered, and reaching out to an unknown. It is risky, fraught with potential failure and personal humiliation, and the ability to facilitate that risk-taking is a central talent of, as Egan says, the skilled manager – in our case, of the manager of students' intellectual, personal and moral growth, the teacher. Lacking those skills will, in both the workplace and the classroom, lead managers in both contexts to face refusal to cooperate, opting out, confrontation and low achievement. What in fact is being resisted is the *danger* people perceive in change; they do not want to appear stupid, incompetent, lacking in skill, so they squat where they are, happy with the familiar, the known and the practised. What the user of counselling skills can do is to communicate *safely* to those under his or her care, leaving them feeling secure that at this time of risk and exposure they will remain respected and valued. 'Rambo' managerial styles, in the classroom or the workplace, simply lock people into self-protective, defensive positions in which creativity dies. So, we elaborate a third key quality of counselling: for therapeutic movement to occur, with the risks involved in that change, counselling *takes place in a relationship where the client feels safe*.

What counsellors can offer, and, significantly, what modern companies are increasingly seeking from them, is an extension and deepening of the skills of interpersonal communication. No less is on offer to teachers. Traditional leadership, both in the business world and in the world of education, has always required competencies specific to the work of the organization: chemicals, medical services, steel, mining, the subject specialisms of the teacher. My own training as a teacher, during the 1960s, concentrated on my ability to 'manage' the language learning of my pupils. My language competence was established via a degree, and my ability to teach them depended on my knowledge of exam syllabi, set texts, knowledge of language acquisition models and so on. I needed to be able to communicate to my pupils (and my head, the parents and other interested bodies) that 'I know this field well; I am trained, an expert; follow me and we will achieve our objectives.' The people with whom I had studied during my university education, by now working for ICI, the National Health Service,

British Steel, British Coal, were engaged in the same communication to their workforce – fundamentally of task competence. Increasingly, while there is no denigration of the skills of the traditional, task-oriented leader, many companies are now asking for more.

They are demanding managerial skill in what has been called 'psycho-social' leadership, which involves the ability to communicate, in addition to the competency message of the traditional leader, a qualitatively different message. All of us as managers are being asked to develop a new set of skills which allow us to communicate to those for whom we have responsibility: 'You know I am task competent in the change we seek. In pursuing this change, I will be concerned about your sense of safety. I will have a developmental view of your work. I will respect you as we pursue this change together. You will not be humiliated, dehumanized or abused. I will try to help you grow as a person.' A bit idealistic? A few years ago I would have thought so, but this is already a theme in managerial training for thousands of employees in the USA and UK, and is beginning to appear in continental Europe. Counsellors are now contributing to the development of psycho-social leadership skills in the world of industry and commerce. All of which brings me to the final specifying characteristic of counselling – it involves the deployment of *a range of techniques and skills, which are used within the client-driven, safe, helping process outlined above* (Figure 3.2).

1. Counselling is a
   relationship
   (safe, client-centred, dynamic)
   within which

2. a range of *skills and techniques*
   are used in order to

3. facilitate a *process* of helping
   positive change
   from dissatisfaction ------------➤ to satisfaction
   pain --------------------➤   comfort
   low esteem ---------------➤   high esteem
   low social skill ------------➤   social skills

Figure 3.2 Counselling: a map of the territory

At the moment we have a fairly general map which tries to structure some of the exploration undertaken above. Given that the word 'counselling' is used with such a variety of meanings, it is important to be precise in suggesting that: (a) all of us in school are involved in the process of helping positive change; and therefore (b) all of us need to be able to some extent to create the facilitative 'counselling' relationship by (c) using the range of skills and techniques of counselling to achieve that change. For the purposes of this text, then, I see counselling to be defined as follows:

> Counselling is a helping process that uses the safety engendered by a
> special kind of relationship to help individuals to get access to a greater
> part of their personal resources, as a means of responding to the

challenges of their life. It uses specific skills and techniques in that relationship to help people become more competent, more contented and more creative. It does not deal primarily with the mentally ill but with normal individuals facing all the difficulties involved in domestic, work-oriented and social life. It is about helping people to grow in emotional fitness and health.

I have tried to parallel the needs of commercial managers and teachers not because I want to commercialize the school (I hope my opening section indicates that the contrary is the case), but because in the bottom-line, accountancy-driven atmosphere in which heads and governing bodies operate, it seems useful to look at the performance enhancement evidence about counselling and its component skills. Rogers (1983) suggests that any human relationship is enhanced or diminished by the presence or absence of the key elements of effective counselling. Thus, it is dispiriting to contrast the decline in the numbers of specialist counsellors working in schools and the paucity of training in basic counselling skills in the initial and post-experience professional development of teachers, with the dramatic, parallel explosion of counselling services for employees offered by some of our largest and most successful companies. As a senior manager or a governor, I would have some probing questions to ask about that paradoxical situation. Our children in schools seem to be receiving less support than their parents receive in their workplaces.

Perhaps some readers will feel that in my attempt to argue the benefits of counselling skills by using some of the current practice in the world of British business, I have strayed too far from the classroom, so let us return there. My own training as a teacher focused on what I have called 'task competence' and 'traditional' leadership skills. I learned to pursue with my pupils academic knowledge, facts, concepts, information and understanding (the plot of *The Brothers Karamazov*, the historical background of Corneille and Racine, the influence of war poetry on political decisions), and was able to develop a number of academic skills (to communicate orally and in writing simple messages in the target language, the ability to draw information from a newspaper, read a text, use a dictionary, write a letter to a pen friend), all related to my 'task competence'. I never specifically paid attention to 'academic attitudes' – the curiosity referred to by Einstein, enthusiasm, love of a subject, willingness to take intellectual risks, to be creative, to be a searcher. On reflection, I would want those qualities to be outcomes of my teaching, but I never analysed how to pursue such goals. Little by little in my professional life I was learning that the classroom is a very complex place indeed, for I realized, as Einstein suggested, that far from promoting those desirable academic attitudes, I was reducing them: killing curiosity, reducing enthusiasm, preventing love of my subject from growing, stifling risk-taking, curiosity and the desire to explore. Of course, some students acquired such attitudes despite me; nor was I maliciously trying to prevent the emergence of such attitudes. I realized that my training was only half complete; although I did not have the vocabulary, I was reaping the harvest of a training regime that offered only 'traditional' leadership skills.

Nor did the complexity of the classroom end with academic attitudes being appended to the pursuit of academic knowledge and skills. It slowly dawned on me that the classroom was teeming with other learning, most of it not scrutinized, accidental in its occurrence and effect. In the social realm, I began to notice that there were lessons of social knowledge (the structure of our society, the role of women, ethnic and cultural minorities), social skills (the merits of collaborative work versus individual work, competition and cooperation, the characteristics of the effective leader or follower) and social attitudes (towards people who are different, towards work, unemployment, industry, politics). None of this learning appeared in lesson notes, lesson plans – rather it emerged as powerful, almost subliminal statements by the group and its teacher via humour, organizational decisions like seating and grouping, selection of materials, response patterns in discussion, consensus and challenge in the class. Significantly, it was rarely subjected to the professional scrutiny of the teacher. I, and I suspect others, were professionals who were unconsciously allowing powerful consequences of our activity, side effects if you like, to occur without control. We were like doctors focusing so tightly on the intended consequences of our medicine that we failed to check carefully the contra-indications. Then, beyond the social learning, deeper and probably more significant, are the emotional lessons we offer our students.

A sense of personal worth is probably the central indicator of mental health (Snygg and Combs, 1959; Jahoda, 1981). 'Mental health' is a concept we as teachers tend to set on one side for the psychiatrists, and perhaps the psychologists, yet we have it thrust under our noses every time a child murders, an adolescent rapes or less sensationally a pupil is deemed anorexic, depressed or anti-social. Like it or not, we are involved in the mental health of our pupils. In his 1967 paper, Daws cites the National Association of Mental Health view that 'school counselling be considered as one potentially valuable contribution to the protection of the mental health of children'. Beyond that protective potential is the challenging concept of the 'pathogenic school', well documented in the literature (McGuiness, 1993a), which indicates that teachers and schools also have a capacity for harm. This will be explored in more detail at the beginning of the next chapter. For me to be ethical in my relationships with my students, I ought to be confident that at least I have done nothing to damage that sense of self-esteem, so crucial to the mental health of the students. As with the academic and social lessons of the classroom, so the emotional ones can be categorized:

- *Emotional knowledge*. How do my pupils learn to answer the question 'who am I?' In my classroom, do they have a realistic awareness of their strengths and weaknesses, do they 'know' themselves?
- *Emotional skill*. Is there opportunity to learn about standpoint taking, value clarification, assertiveness skills, delay of gratification, temper control? What kind of a model am I, the teacher?
- *Emotional attitudes*. Do self-acceptance, a sense of responsibility, respect for others infuse the ambience of the classroom?

It would be possible to continue analysing just how complex the demands made on teachers are; for example, what moral knowledge, skills and attitudes infuse my classroom, or what do my students learn about sexuality? My intention has been to indicate that in addition to the academic parts of my work there is a matrix of other learning which demands careful analysis, and the teacher's response to that analysis will involve the deployment of the skills of the psycho-social leader.

Elsewhere (McGuiness, 1982, 1988), there are detailed accounts of an increasingly performed exercise used to explore some of the fundamental principles outlined above. It appears, for those who want to use it, at the end of this chapter. The 'bad–good teacher' analysis consistently reveals that students, practising teachers, social workers, careers officers, business managers, inspectors and health professionals, having been asked to draw to mind a teacher or professional mentor about whom they would say, 'this person damaged me, reduced my potential, failed to develop my talent', select *interpersonal characteristics* as the most significant influence on their perception of the bad teacher. It is rare that an academic or intellectual deficiency is highlighted. In the second stage of the exercise, the group is asked to reflect on the impact of a teacher about whom they would say, 'this teacher raised my sights, helped me develop talents I didn't know I had, gave me a sense of purpose and direction' – the good teacher. Again, the groups without fail identify the warmth, the enthusiasm, the acceptance, the respect, the interpersonal sensitivity of the teacher. They are not of course devaluing the academic skills of the teacher, or suggesting that the knowledge base of the profession is insignificant; but they are saying with great emphasis that however *knowledgeable* the teacher, deficiency in interpersonal skills or intrapersonal stability and comfort destroys effective teaching. Thus as teachers, we need enhanced interpersonal skills and increased self-awareness and acceptance – two key foci of counsellor training.

To the best of my knowledge there is no 'code of ethics' for British teachers. We are, of course, subject to the law that governs the health and safety of pupils in school, those laws that protect all of us from abuse and danger, and the legal dimensions of what it is to be *in loco parentis*. But ethical codes? As a psychologist I am governed by the code of the British Psychological Society; the British Association for Counselling has its members practise under the 1992 Code of Ethics and Practice for Counsellors. Nurses have them, with the basic exhortation of Florence Nightingale that they 'should do the patient no harm'; doctors, too, in their Hippocratic oath state that wherever they go to treat patients, they 'will enter only for the good of my patients keeping myself far from all intentional ill doing'. Typically, ethical codes go further than simply requiring professionals not to harm clients; they place on their members an obligation, among others, to stay up to date, informed on the current state of best practice. and to undertake constant professional development. Kitchener (1984) describes an 'intuitive' level of ethics that we bring to our professional activity: the gut reactions, born of the beliefs, knowledge and assumptions we have accumulated over the years. I recall with a shudder taking a group of teacher trainees to a host school to meet their mentor. 'Just remember one thing,' he said, offering an ingrained, intuitive ethical position. 'All kids are liars.' Fortunately, such negative intuitive positions are rare, but the anecdote offers a salutary reminder that, as Kitchener goes on to argue, our intuitive positions need to be scrutinized against a number of fundamental ethical principles. These include an acceptance of personal autonomy and responsibility, commitment to the same characteristics in those for whom we work, our students, and finally a principle of 'non-malificence', which means a commitment to take steps not to harm those in our care.

It will be clear to the reader that two related but distinct patterns are beginning to emerge. There is first an argument to be pursued that *all* teachers need highly developed interpersonal characteristics, which are also the foundation characteristics of the effective counsellor. Consequent upon the establishment and acceptance of that position is an ethical requirement, i.e. the identification of what those characteristics are and how they might be developed. There is another dimension to be explored. Despite the need for, and increasing skill in, basic counselling among classroom teachers, there are cases to be responded to in school that require levels of expertise or quantities of time that the ordinary teacher does not have. For such cases schools and their pupils need access to specialist counsellors. Here again, we parallel the managers in the world of commerce. They need (so the argument goes) highly developed interpersonal characteristics to facilitate day-to-day pursuit of the organization's tasks, *and* they need referral points to which employees with specific challenges can be directed.

As I mentioned in Chapter 2, our task as teachers can be viewed as one of 'managing' the complex, exciting and challenging changes that our students face – as Rogers suggested, the excitement of *both* intellectual and emotional discovery. We are managers of change no less than the IBM manager or the Unilever manager, and just as they need to hone skills in interpersonal sensitivity as well as expertise in information technology or industrial chemistry, so we teachers must explore beyond our subject specialism into the realm of interpersonal communication. Given the powerful lobby (Lawlor *et al.*) that seeks to strip the education of our pupils to some cheap, utilitarian skeleton, it does seem worthwhile to reiterate the *commercially driven* moves in the world of work towards a large and increasing demand for counsellors to help managers to develop basic counselling skills, as well as a huge increase in the employment of specialist counsellors in the workplace. In 1990, Sutherland and Cooper could make this criticism of the industrial and commercial world:

> We constantly hear chief executives, personnel executives, government administrators, hospital administrators, headmasters [*sic*], and others in authority roles extolling the fact that the most important resource they have is people. Yet when it comes right down to it, how often do organisations protect, support and nurture this most valuable asset, the human resource? (p. 253)

The change in attitudes towards the human resource, people in organizations, during the past five years has been remarkable. To some extent, extension of health and safety at work provision to include social and emotional issues has led some organizations to a self-protective posture designed to pre-empt litigation by damaged employees. But there is also a realization in large companies that employees are genuinely valuable, expensively trained *investments*. As machines undergo a daily maintenance check in a local factory, it is intriguing to reflect on how often, as we streamed into school for another tiring day, if we were machines undergoing that same check, the technician would ring the head: 'Sorry, Joe Smith and Mary Brown are on the blink today. I'll have to take them out for a full service.' No, the human machines, pupils and staff, grind on in self-destructive, inefficient and possibly dangerous survival modes – the expendable human resource. Just as companies are now questioning that wasteful and dehumanizing approach, so in schools we might begin to look beyond the structures of our pastoral care systems to the high level of professional skills that the rhetoric of those systems requires.

The move towards enhancing the socio-emotional environment of the workplace and much greater provision of counselling services in large companies has paradoxically and sadly been paralleled by a simultaneous disappearance of the school-based counsellor. It seems that we are in the barely ethical situation of no longer being able to afford provision for our pupils of the kind of care and protection now made available to large numbers of the adult workforce. An article in the *Times Educational Supplement* (7 October 1994) said that the British Association for Counselling had 300 members working with children under 16, but since that included youth workers and Education Welfare Officers (EWOs), the number working specifically as school counsellors was tiny. Schools have consciously responded to some of the research findings cited above by increasing the amount of in-service training of willing teachers in 'counselling skills', thus enhancing the 'socio-emotional climate of the workplace', and this is a very positive step forward. It is significant, though, that despite the recommendation of the Elton Report (1989, R.43) that all teacher trainees should be introduced to basic counselling skills, the new regulations on initial teacher training make no provision for it.

Without apology I will close this chapter by referring back to the world of commerce. In Sutherland and Cooper's comment cited above, they are lamenting the absence of psycho-social leadership skills, the failure to implant in the organization a vision of human beings as of intrinsic value, the blindness of senior managers to the need for what Egan (1993) referred to as 'a culture of vigilance', a protective posture towards employees – in practical terms, a lack of basic counselling skills in the workplace, and a consequent reduction of productivity and wastage of talent. Much has changed in the business world in the past five years, despite a recession; schools should not lag behind.

Exercises

This chapter has argued that the task of the teacher goes beyond the limited vision of 'theorists' like Lawlor (1990), which constrains teachers to the more basic role of 'instructors', suggesting that even without the philosophical position that we are educators of the whole child, psychological theory strongly indicates that mere instruction is impossible. All human interaction produces socio-emotional as well as cognitive reactions. This interaction can be random, haphazard, as apparently Lawlor accepts, or considered, analysed, taken into account in planning, as any professional would expect. These exercises will explore the complex dynamic of our activity in classrooms.

The bad, the good and where is Clint Eastwood?

The chapter mentions the extensive use of this exercise, which is used to increase awareness of the importance of interpersonal issues in all professional work with human beings, including medicine, management, social work, policing, customs and excise, and education. The focus here will be on teaching.

Dig back into your past, recent or distant, and try to pull into your mind the memory of a teacher about whom you would say, 'That person diminished me, humiliated me, reduced my effectiveness, was in some sense destructive in her or his impact on me.' Recall, in as much detail as you can, experiences of that effect – not just what happened, but your reaction, as fully as possible.

It is important to help participants to experience the socio-emotional impact as well as the more controlled intellectual impact.

Now, imagine that your partner is that person. In two minutes share your reaction – not as a memory, this is your tormentor. 'You damaged me when . . ., I felt . . ., I look back at you as . . .' Each take a turn, then collect on a large sheet of paper, for later sharing, nouns, adjectives and verbs that catch the flavour of the two persons recalled. When that is completed, can you now draw to mind an entirely different kind of person: some teacher about whom you would say, 'She or he was special, enhanced my aspirations, helped me to grow, develop, helped me to learn.' Again, in turns, imagine that your partner is your admired mentor, and in the here-and-now speak: 'I learned so much with you, you always . . . I particularly liked . . .' Collect the characteristics of the positive teacher, and again catch the flavour of the person. A display of the charts of the various pairs in the group will form the basis of a discussion.

The descriptors can be grouped: those relating to task leadership and those relating to social leadership; or interpersonal dimensions and academic dimensions; or instructor skills and teacher skills. The usual finding is that we identify the interpersonal dimensions as foundational, a *sine qua non* for the effective teacher. Of course, we need our academic competence, but that drains away like water into sand if it is not mediated to pupils in an ambience of interpersonal respect.

Where do I go from here? A self-audit

Returning to the lists of characteristics of bad and good teachers generated in the previous exercise, we can find challenging material for use in our own professional development. I find that I have a tendency to link the 'bad' list generated by group members with my own former bad experiences in school, or even with some current colleagues. More productive, though requiring more discipline, is to check to see to what extent the elements in the bad list slip into my work.

Using either the lists of you and your partner, or a composite of all the lists generated by the group, give yourself a score out of ten on each of the qualities identified: zero means that quality does not exist at all in your interpersonal style; ten means you communicate it to a very high degree. Do this with both the negative and the positive list, then discuss the implications for teaching and professional development with your partner, e.g.

Destructive	Positive
sarcasm (3)	gives time (8)
humiliates (0)	listens (8)
bullies (2)	encourages (9)
sexist (5)	enthusiasm (5)
makes people feel small (1)	caring (7)
arrogant (2)	likes people (8)
defensive (3)	good at subject (9)
distant (2)	friendly (9)

The trainer may want to point out the similarities in the replies given by managers, nurses, doctors, social workers and so on. To be effective in task leadership, we also need the skills of the psycho-social leader. People will not change when they are scared; they are too busy protecting themselves.

Rabbie Burns's giftie

To see ourselves as others see us, a frightening thought! The following exercise needs lots of humour, openness and trust in the group. Trainers will judge when it is opportune. I may see myself as an effective 'psycho-social leader', while others have a completely different view of me.

If there are twelve in the group, sub-divide into two groups of six, A and B, with each member of a sub-group finding a partner in the other sub-group. Group A then forms a circle (see Figure 3.3) and the members of group B place themselves so that they can see their partners in group A clearly. Tell the groups that the roles will be reversed in the second fifteen minutes. The Bs will be given an observation protocol to assist their analysis of what happens. The trainer will place a sealed envelope on the floor in the centre of the group, and when all are in position, say, 'Your task for the next fifteen minutes is written on a paper inside the envelope. You can begin now. Will group B members observe the interpersonal processes of the group.' In the envelope will be a task related to some topical issue, e.g. create on a flip-chart an argument that teachers are best trained entirely in schools, or that modern languages for all pupils is not a realistic educational objective, or your own task. The task needs to be mildly polemical. It may add spice if the trainer creates a little pressure by saying from time to time, 'You are half-way through the time . . . only five minutes to go', etc. When the fifteen minutes are up, change roles and repeat the process, either with a new task or, if it seems still to have a spark, with the same task. But start with it closed, in the envelope, to get the group dynamic going. A final discussion can explore any surprises, bits of personal learning, insights gained. Relate the whole exercise to teaching and counselling.

For the observers (bear in mind that you will be observed as well, so try to be accurate but constructive)

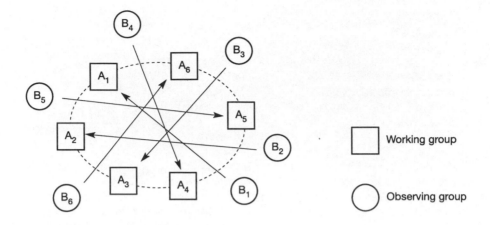

Figure 3.3 Goldfish bowl exercise

General:

- *Who took the initiative, picked up the envelope, opened it? What was the dynamic for this? The reaction of your partner?*
- *Has anyone dropped out? Decided the exercise is too frivolous (or threatening)? How is that evident?*
- *Is anyone clearly exercising 'social leadership skills'? Or 'task leadership skills'?*

Detail:

Evidence (what she or he is doing) of

Task leader	*Social leader*
organizing	*listening*
informing	*summarizing*
explaining	*paraphrasing*
directing	*creating space for others' contribution*
planning	*coordinating*
time concern	*establishing safety*
task focus	*involving others*
egocentric	*unselfish*
initiator	*reconciler*
meet the deadline	*climate creator*

These are not judgemental categories; they describe behaviours you observe, and become the basis for a discussion about 'my' interpersonal style. I can say to my partner, 'This is what I saw, what do you make of that?' If you were organizing a large party, would you choose someone who scored high on the first column or the second; if you were feeling down, would you want to talk to the same kind of person or not? We need both types of skill, and ideally, we need them both in the same person.

CHAPTER 4

All change: a profile of counselling

Donald Blocher (1974) introduced me to a character in a Piazza novel. A 12-year-old boy, reflecting, as adolescents will, on the complexity of life, says, 'Funny how things change so sudden. Things can be one way today, and the next day be the very opposite. That is the exact and very strange truth.' In a couple of sentences, Alexander crystallizes the challenging nature of life: today a child, tomorrow a young adult; today a spouse, tomorrow a widow or widower; today an employee, tomorrow redundant; today a student, tomorrow in the labour market. Each of us can list the changes we have experienced in our life, and we can categorize them: the ones we sailed through, the ones that left us anxious and puzzled, the ones that were exhilarating, the ones that wounded us deeply, the ones we wanted to tackle alone and the ones where we received welcome help. And there are some we faced alone, desperate for help that never arrived. I remember talking with a student, a victim for years of sexual abuse, and hearing her tell of her attempts to seek help from teachers. What could she say, at 12 years old, in the days that preceded the sensitivity and availability of help we have today? 'My Dad has sex with me'? Hardly. She approached her cry for help tangentially, testing the capability of the teacher, feeling puzzled and hurt herself, and wondering subliminally if this teacher would be strong enough to help. The slightest rebuff would block her, lock her into her own private pain. She described in tears how no one picked up her distress signals, or if they did, they were shocked into a discreet withdrawal. Today a child, an innocent, tomorrow a victim of rape.

Hufton (1986) surveyed secondary school children's experience of loss, and their response to that challenge. She found that the pupils' perception of loss (death of parents, siblings, grandparents, friends, even pets) was much more pervasive than she had expected, and that the impact of the loss was much more traumatic than the sparse literature suggested. Some children in the interviews included such things as the loss consequent upon divorce or parental imprisonment – it was a whole area to which I as a teacher had paid minimal attention, beyond a basic response to family bereavement. Significantly, the pupils overwhelmingly said they would have liked to have had some support from their school, and in large numbers said that it was not available. Beyond the specialist support available via bereavement counselling, these children needed sensitively deployed counselling skills from subject teachers, who would act both as caring support staff and, where necessary, as referral agents.

This is not in any sense an attempt to bash teachers. I include myself, in my days as a language teacher, as one of those who was simply not sensitized to the complex, layered nature of supporting students in school. To return to the parallel drawn with other working environments, McGuiness (1993c) writes of the impact the kind of changes outlined above have on workers:

> The impact [of these changes] on their work is frequently covert, only emerging when the industrial accident, the sales disaster, the faulty project-costing throws into high profile a client who needed help and did not get it. The provision of a counselling service is a natural extension of the health and safety at work legislation, and it speaks volumes of the attitude of an employer to the workforce. (p. 3)

No less is the case in the classroom: the strong impact of the challenge of change on pupils, frequently with covert effects, emerging only when faulty performance (academic, behavioural) puts it on to an overt agenda. Bishop (1990) summarizes it thus, arguing from his experience as a deputy head that we need 'someone who can act as a support to an already existing pastoral system, which seeks primarily to be preventative rather than remedial, but which is realistic enough to admit that at times serious problems do arise, and that help is required.'

The help that is required is the help offered in counselling, and it seems appropriate, having argued for both a specialist and a generalist competency to be available to pupils in school, to move into a detailed analysis of the map presented in Chapter 3. We need to analyse counselling in great detail, and to draw from that analysis the kind of professional development needed by both the generalist and the specialized practitioner.

We have already considered Eysenck's (1953) series of highly critical comments on counselling. At least he performed the useful service of forcing us to ask the question: does counselling work? His disparaging use of the term 'the talking cure' was a challenge to the counselling community to take an evaluative pause for breath. Eysenck had analysed hundreds of outcome studies of neurotic clients and concluded that counselling was no more effective in producing positive change than was the effect of time or spontaneous remission. Counsellors, it seemed, were to be reduced to the status of 'symptom relievers', while time did its work – the analgesic effect. Rogers (1951) had made strong claims for the existence of an empirical base which supported a claim for the effectiveness of counselling. He accepted that 'the researches have had definite and often serious limitations' (p. 12), but their methodology would permit 'any competent worker to verify the findings, either by re-studying the same case material or by using the same method on new material' (p. 13). Eysenck took up the challenge, and drew the conclusion outlined above.

The debate about efficacy continues, and Herr (1976) makes the astute comment that to ask 'does counselling work?' is not to pose a researchable question. We might as well ask: does teaching work, or does medicine work? As we have seen, the danger of an averaging effect led Truax and Carkhuff (1967) to disaggregate the global figures of Eysenck, reanalyse the data and conclude that he 'was essentially correct in saying that average counselling and psychotherapy as it is currently practised does not result in average client improvement greater than that observed in clients who received no special counselling or psychotherapeutic treatment' (p. 5). Thus, in average terms, Eysenck was right: counselling was a neutral, ineffective activity. However, before readers decide to cut their losses now, throw this book away and head off for the pub, Truax and Carkhuff did identify a significant new element: within the global accuracy of Eysenck's figures (of nil effect), some individual counsellors were producing highly effective outcomes. The shadow of that, of course, is that given the general accuracy, if some counsellors were effective beyond the neutral average, others must have been ineffective to a degree that led their clients to recover at rates below the spontaneous remission rates. The concept of the effective counsellor and the concept of the counsellor who harms were born.

Carkhuff and Berenson (1977), developing this theme, commented that teacher–student, parent–child and counsellor–client relationships 'may have constructive or deteriorative effects on intellectual as well as emotional functioning' (p. 38). They stick us firmly into the demands of ethical teaching, explored in Chapter 3: if our activities have a capacity for harming others, then we have an ethical, professional obligation to scrutinize them with that possibility in mind. A clear consequence of the initial findings of Truax and Carkhuff was the need to sift through the practice of both successful and unsuccessful counsellors to identify those qualities and skills that correlated with successful client outcomes.

COUNSELLING: THE SPECIAL RELATIONSHIP

This focus of research, for the central qualities of the successful counsellor, has reinforced the very early statements of Rogers (1942) that the quality of the relationship is the key to positive change in the client. What Truax and Carkhuff (1967) found was that the presence of a number of what are called 'core conditions' for effective counselling determined the extent of client improvement. Strupp (1986) sheds more light, offering both structure and a clear indication of the complexity of the task:

> the therapist's skill is significantly manifested by an ability to create a particular interpersonal context, and within that context, to foster certain kinds of learning. In other words the therapist may be said to develop, maintain and manage a specialised human relationship with therapeutic intent. The goal is to promote learning within a benign and constructive interpersonal context. (p. 122)

Perhaps most succinctly, we find Norcross and Guy (1989) rejecting the 'tyranny of technique' and the 'myth of disembodied treatment', and asserting that 'the psychotherapist is the central determinant of clinical improvement', i.e. it is not the technique, the activity, that is primary, it is the nature of the *person* who offers the help that underpins the process. Brammer and Shostrum (1982) summarize the available evidence to conclude that all the major theories and schools of counselling, with their different skills and techniques, produce positive outcomes. The major influence is the quality of the relationship within which these skills are deployed. It is not primarily what I do, it is who I am in the relationship.

So what do we know about the qualities of this person and the kind of relationship she or he needs to create? (The reader may find it useful to link the findings on the primacy of the relationship over technique with the exploration of task and social leadership skills in Chapter 3.)

Any human relationship – being a son or daughter, a parent, a teacher, a friend, a spouse, a manager – is affected for good or ill by the presence or absence of what are now commonly designated the 'core dimensions' (Rogers, 1942, 1951, 1983; Truax and Carkhuff, 1967). They are:

- empathy;
- unconditional positive regard;
- genuineness;
- immediacy.

These core conditions for effective therapy, explored in detail by Truax and Carkhuff (1968) and Carkhuff and Berenson (1977), take us on a journey into the heart of social leadership skills (for the teacher and manager) and therapeutic skills (for the counsellor). There is nothing 'magical' or charismatic about them; they exist on the same 'human interaction continuum' and are capable of development in training. We use them in varying degrees in all our interactions with other human beings. What the counsellor is required to do, is to hone them to a highly developed professional extent beyond the normal use we make of them. Nor can we 'play-act', dissimulate, pretend the presence of these qualities. The communication of the core conditions must be quintessentially honest. Therein lies the challenge. The research is clear that without the presence of these 'core dimensions', *all* of our interactive behaviour is diminished in its effectiveness.

Empathy involves the ability to merge in some sense with the client's perception, accepting it as authentic. In some way, we can become able to experience that perception, suspending our own perceptual experience to give full attention to our client's reality. It requires me to 'be' where my client is, and at the same time to avoid becoming entangled in whatever rigidities or inflexibilities are blocking the client's way forward. It is non-judgemental, non-evaluative: a clear statement to the client that the material to be considered is his or hers; that my agenda has no significance in the encounter. It is a statement of respect towards the client, about accepting the reality that only the client is in full possession of, and which contains the significant elements to be worked through. My attempts to be the expert, to race ahead to *my* solution, must be put on one side, in the certainty that I am not equipped to solve someone else's problem. Rogers (1951) puts it thus: 'as the client is genuinely exploring the unknown, the counsellor becomes wholly engaged in trying to keep step with this puzzled and puzzling search. His attention is completely focussed upon the attempt to perceive from the client's frame of reference' (p. 112). The techniques and skills which allow us to achieve that focus will be presented later, but we can see clearly that they run counter to much conventional wisdom, e.g. that I can somehow solve my client's problem. Prior to the techniques lies a filter of personal values about status, power, competence, control, and so on, which will influence *who I am* in the relationship – as we have seen, a significantly more powerful influence than what I do. An example may illustrate the point clearly – it is an example of my own incompetence, whose only positive consequence may be its illustrative power here! Having spent several months working, in my view unsuccessfully, with someone suffering from an eating disorder, and with my perception of my own competence under some stress and a faulty view of my own status in the encounter, I tried to control the direction of the counselling by interjecting at what seemed to me an appropriate point, 'You know, I read in an article today that 60 per cent of sufferers from eating disorders have been sexually abused.' My agenda, my attempt to be the expert, my attempt to control the direction of the encounter – whatever else I was doing, it was not counselling. I was working with my perceptual field, not my client's. My client replied immediately, 'Well, I must be in the other 40 per cent.' When, weeks later, she disclosed that she had in fact been sexually abused, I recalled her earlier statement. 'It wasn't time to talk about it,' she said. Her perceptual field, her reality, her control. My inopportune, frustrated intervention had done no more than block her. I had tried to subvert the 'wisdom of the client', and inevitably had failed.

Unconditional positive regard fundamentally involves the counsellor in being able to communicate to the client that he or she is accepted as having a core of inviolable dignity and value – that no matter what, at the centre of our relationship is an acceptance of the person which is beyond challenge. Clients can be hostile towards us, demeaning, downright rude, but the unconditional regard required of the counsellor means that we accept what the client gives, and work with that. we do not judge, we accept. This is Rogers in 1942:

> As a person talks about himself . . . where there is no necessity to defend himself, the real issues become more and more evident to the observant listener . . . Consequently the best techniques for interviewing are those which encourage the client to express himself as freely as possible, with the counsellor consciously endeavouring to refrain from any activity or any response which would guide the direction of the interview or the content brought forward. (pp. 132–3)

He reminds us that questioning the client may produce key material, but at a cost in terms of time, and with the danger that the difficulties uncovered may be difficulties of the counsellor, not the client! The ability to communicate unconditional positive regard contributes powerfully to the client's growing feeling of safety; in this context, the client can explore, search, 'be myself fully', scrutinize that self without needing to set up internal and external barriers and protections to ensure its safety.

Genuineness requires the counsellor to be able to communicate with the client in a way which, to use Rogers's phrase, is transparent. The communication in the relationship should involve no, or minimal, conflict between the counsellor's own, total experience and awareness and her or his overt communication with the client. I should disclose what is happening to me in the encounter, with great sensitivity towards and awareness of what is happening. The counsellor must learn to enhance her or his self-awareness to ensure that self-disclosure is very accurate. Thus, in a group therapy session, one member said, 'I feel very threatened by Mandy's constant silence; she doesn't give, she just seems to watch us all.' (The surface message: I am threatened by your selfish observation of me.) Later, after some group discussion, the person said, 'I still feel what I said, but I also feel good that Mandy doesn't feel pressured to talk; and I look forward to when she will be able to share with us.' There are three messages instead of the one that was closest to the surface. (I am still feeling threatened, *and* I am pleased that Mandy is not feeling pressured, *and* I hope she will share as we spend more time in the group.) There is greater self-awareness, greater ability to communicate that awareness. Though that occurred in a group context, it does draw attention to the fact that genuineness is not some invitation to the counsellor to sound off at the client. Our values need to be clarified: who am I, from the point of view of values, in an encounter that involves questions of authority, sexuality, death, relationships, property, loyalty, solitude? What is the baggage that I drag, perhaps unconsciously, into the process? Again, being genuine sounds straightforward, but it can make heavy demands on us if we bring into our encounters with others personal material that we have never processed. Returning to the insight from Rogers in the previous paragraph, the difficulties uncovered may belong to the counsellor, not the client.

Immediacy takes us back towards awareness. It involves a highly developed sensitivity towards the here-and-now. Perls (1973) in particular, and gestalt therapists in general, emphasize the concept of 'wholeness' in the therapeutic encounter. I am not simply a 'head', an intellect, who goes into encounters with other people; I take into a counselling session, a classroom, a dinner party, my sensations, my aches and pains, my euphorias, my depressions, my body. Nor is my client a 'mouth'. She or he too comes in a body that aches, or feels good, with delights and miseries at an emotional level, with tastes in the mouth and perfumes in the nose, with tactile and visual awarenesses. Our wholeness is in contact, whether we advert to it or not, and if not, then the immediacy of the encounter is diminished. How aware am I at this moment? Two seconds ago, I was thinking; now I am aware of the warmth of the fire on my right side, an ache there too (bad posture at the word processor?), some delight at the prospect of lunch with friends, a sensation of pressure at how slowly the writing is going – and so on. All of that is me, not just coordinating fingers and brain via a word processor. So with clients: often access to important material is gained not by our intellects; they are well practised in defence, denial, rationalization and so on. We can find ourselves, and help our clients to do so, by enhancing our sensitivity to the other parts of our being that speak constantly, but are frequently ignored. Who are we in this encounter, in the here-and-now?

Not only do these characteristics control the success or otherwise of counselling encounters, they also, as Rogers's (1983) text argues, have a crucial impact on the classroom. While it may be challenging to accept the idea in theory, a more important insight for me comes from my experience that those teachers from whom I learned most as a new entrant into the profession, who filled me with admiration and envy of their skill with pupils, in fact communicated the elements described above to their pupils. They were gifted in being able to enter the world of their students, not in some patronizing way that demeaned both them and their students, but *empathically*, so that they had a real sense of the phenomenological world that their students inhabited. Equally, they were able to communicate to their students that, no matter what, they were on their side; there was a sense of commitment, support, close attention that in counselling is called *unconditional positive regard*. Nor did they pretend to their students – they were open, challenging, honest, *genuine* and, most of all, themselves. They felt no need to hide behind facades or self-protective strategies; they understood, at least implicitly, that they had to present a full 'self' if they were to encourage the students to disclose their full selves. And they were *immediate*. They had a sensitivity to the here-and-now that left pupils wondering if they had some kind of magic powers. What the pupils learned from the communication of that degree of detailed attention was that they mattered, and mattered greatly. It is not at all surprising that the exercise described in Chapter 3 draws from participants, in a less formal language, that 'good teachers' communicate empathy, unconditional positive regard, genuineness and immediacy, while 'destructive' teachers communicate distance, disrespect and sometimes contempt, facades and lack of interest or awareness in the 'now' of an encounter. It is exactly what Truax and Carkhuff found in the case of successful and unsuccessful counsellors: successful human interaction correlates closely with the extent to which that interaction takes place in a relationship infused by the core conditions.

There are, of course, just as Truax and Carkhuff found in analysing the qualities of successful and harmful counsellors, successful and destructive teachers. The 'good–bad teacher' exercise reveals that most participants have experienced being in the classroom of someone they now regard as having had a destructive effect on their development. That, for me as a teacher, is a very sobering thought. More disquieting is my experience as a counsellor trainer. When, in learning how to facilitate a client's moving into deeper, more buried material, trainees are asked to try to access something personal of great significance in their development, and which they are willing, in the somewhat artificial setting of the training programme, to share, with startling frequency they select hurtful experiences from school – now buried, but still rumbling away after all those years. They use words like 'humiliation', 'ridicule' and 'contempt' to describe feelings they thought were long gone. They are in fact describing relationships in which the core conditions for effective relating were non-existent. At the very least, as teachers we ought to explore our ability to establish a relationship infused by the core conditions, one that offers to our students safety, respect for their autonomy and the dynamism of challenge.

COUNSELLING: THE PROCESS

I remember my first lesson plan: immaculate; location of the lesson in the scheme of work; teaching objectives; operational objectives; materials and equipment needed; introductory five minutes, make it enjoyable; presentation of the material; test orally; re-present; written exercise; final 'jolly', leave them happy; off to mark the written work. It was so tidy and predictable, and in my innocence I thought that that was how it would happen! Fortunately, the classroom is a much messier and more challenging place than my inexperience anticipated. The process I had carefully mapped out was, could be, no more than a map, a framework. So it must be with the process of counselling.

The 'lesson plan' approach suggests that counselling takes place in three basic phases (Egan, 1986) which occur in a linear, sequential way. Of course the reality is more complex, but let us use the analysis to gain a foothold in the process. Initially, there is an *exploratory phase*, in which the counsellor tries to help the client to gain access to the real challenge. Often, there is a 'presenting problem' which the client uses to get a purchase on something more profound, more taxing. The presenting problem can also be used, even unconsciously, as a 'test' for the counsellor. Will this person really offer me the kind of safe-dynamic climate in which I can really explore key material? Can this person create for me, the client, a counselling relationship in the sense described above? The client is helped to perceive herself or himself in greater depth and with greater accuracy than previously. That is a frightening thing to do, and most people do it very slowly, only in relationships that feel very safe. Then, when the client, having explored carefully, courageously, is able to say, 'yes, that is what I want to tackle', the process moves to what is called the *understanding* or *insight phase*. In this phase, the client is helped to view her or his perception less rigidly, to walk around a previously intractable problem, achieving new, potentially more productive perspectives. This will frequently involve helping the client to work with the deeper material of values, feelings and attitudes. Together, client and counsellor will know that this stage is almost complete when the counsellor is able to make this type of comment accurately: 'When we started, I remember you saying that the thing that was most bothering you was X [the end of the exploratory phase], and I think that you are now saying that what you want to do about it is Y [the end of the understanding phase].' The client may say, 'Yes, that's what I would really *like* to do, but I don't know how/can't', and take us very clearly into the third part of the process, the *action phase*. The title is self-explanatory – it is the phase in which the counsellor helps the client to plan, implement and evaluate client-chosen strategies for emerging successfully from the challenge identified in phase one. It expands the coping repertoire of the client to include behaviours that previously seemed out of reach. Of course, the process is not as clinical and predictable as this – as with lesson-planning there will be overlap and returns to earlier parts of the process – but the framework does offer us a model in which to analyse in detail the activity of the counsellor.

One of the axioms of good teaching that has stayed with me right through work with primary school children, secondary pupils, undergraduate, post-graduate, doctoral and post-doctoral students is that there is no point in the teacher answering questions that the learner is not asking. For example, long ago, picking up a science lesson from an absent colleague, I discovered that we were to analyse soil. I had a list of the constituents we would expect to find using the various laboratory techniques at our disposal – I could have given the list, to be learned by heart, thus providing answers to questions the class were not asking. What I needed was some way of getting them curious (Einstein again), and I was delighted when someone introduced the topic of being buried alive. Was air a constituent of soil? If so, how much was there, and did it vary in different soils? Was there good soil for being buried in? What would its characteristics be? Precisely how much air was there in the clump of soil we had, and what else was there? We were off. Teacher readers will have myriad examples, and better ones, to illustrate the point that before mastering and understanding material, we need to give it our real attention, we need to engage it. So it is in the process of counselling.

A client, a pupil, will have some issue, a personal challenge or difficulty, to respond to. It can be apparently straightforward to the teacher or counsellor, but they maintain an awareness of the need to empathize, accepting the pupil's perception of the gravity of the situation. The fact that Tom Brown is in agonies that he has not yet got pubic hair, when everyone else in the team has, may be a cause for humour among his peers and perhaps his teachers if they knew, but for Tom, in his perceptual field, it is catastrophic. His failure to turn up for training, insistence on going home filthy after the game, may lead to speculation about causes, but in the final analysis, he needs the space, safety and confidence to talk without fear of ridicule. Rogers (1951) himself makes this comment: 'I have feared that if I allow some of the more tender parts of me to become exposed in the therapeutic relationship, they would be trampled on, misused and perhaps ridiculed' (p.160). If that is how Rogers felt, imagine the agonies of our pupils as they try to share their 'more tender parts.' Of course, a little time may solve this particular problem, and Tom may never need to have recourse to a teacher, but our initial awareness of a difficulty and our communication of the core conditions are the starting point for help, when and if the pupil seeks it.

EXPLORATION

The initial contact in the process is the presentation of the problem. Intuitively we know as teachers that pupils will approach us ostensibly to talk about one issue, when they really want to tackle something much deeper: the 'Sir/miss, I've got this friend who . . . ' syndrome. Sometimes the real issue is not very apparent, even to the pupil – she or he is in exploratory mode. Sometimes time, at other times impatience or a feeling that we can get this sorted out before break ends, can lead us to a premature presumption that the presenting problem is 'it'. The pupil is unconsciously saying, 'I've got this thing niggling away at me, and I've found this way in to talk about it' – a beginning, difficult but possible – and suddenly he or she is outside with the 'presenting problem' sorted, and the door closed on wherever an exploration might have led. This example may illustrate the idea. I received a knock on my door, to find a student waiting, rather solemn-looking. 'Hi, David, what can I do for you? (What follow are the bones of a twenty-minute conversation.)

'I'd like to switch from Spanish to Italian' (presenting problem – no problem, a few forms to fill, a couple of phone calls). As a counsellor, I need to be working on the core conditions, creating a safe, student-controlled relationship: empathy, unconditional positive regard, genuineness, immediacy; open to the possibility that the subject switch is 'an entrance' to something he finds more worrying, but in no way presuming that to be the case.

'The Spanish isn't too attractive for you, then?' An attempt to empathize: is this where you are, am I getting hold of what you're saying accurately? Also a statement of his value, my unconditional positive regard for him: I want to listen, not jump in with a solution, before we really know what the challenge is.

'It's not so much that. I quite like it – I just want to change to Italian.' My empathic statement is refined by him. Must stay with him, not interrogating, just staying where I think he is.

'So, you say you quite like the Spanish, and that you want to change to Italian. I'm not sure I'm with you.' Empathize – give him back the 'paradoxical' entrance he is hovering at. Again, not evaluating or criticizing, simply staying with him.

'I know, that sounds daft, doesn't it' (he does his own evaluating). 'You see, Laura [his girlfriend, whom I know] and I have split up, and she's got this other guy in Spanish. They sit holding hands, and smiling at each other . . . '

A request to change his subject of study is rapidly explored to reveal a broken relationship as the real issue. What David is looking for is a way of coming to terms with the pain involved in the end of a relationship. By reflecting that back to him, and his acceptance of that as an accurate reflection of where he really was, we began to explore together his real challenge.

At the risk of over-simplification, the purpose of the exploratory stage of counselling can be said to be the part of the process in which we help our client to arrive at a point where she or he is able to respond affirmatively to the counsellor's reflective statement: 'So, listening to what you say, you seem to be saying that what is really bothering you at the moment is . . . ' It is like good teaching: before launching into loads of answers, we first need to establish the questions. Nor will the process of counselling continue in a strictly linear way. We may think we have the issue, and then found that we are exploring again – a refinement of the issue. David may set off exploring his broken relationship with Laura and the hurt he is feeling from that, only to discover, deeper, some unresolved pain from a bereavement suffered when he was a child. We *cannot* know, and will only find out by making the journey of exploration with the client in the lead. Once more Rogers (1951) describes the process with great precision:

> In this attempt to struggle along with the client, to glimpse with him the half understood causes of behaviour, to wrestle with feelings which emerge into awareness and then slip away again, it is entirely possible that 'an accurate reflection of feeling' no longer fits the therapist's behaviour. Rather than serving as a mirror, the therapist becomes a companion to the client as the latter searches through a tangled forest in the dead of night. The therapist's responses are more in the nature of calls through the darkness: Am I with you? Is this where you are? Are we together? Is this the direction you are heading? (p.113)

UNDERSTANDING AND INSIGHT

One of the characteristics of our response to danger is that we concentrate on the perceived threat – we lock on to it, in order to be fully cognizant of its potential to destroy us. We withdraw our attention from those stimuli which seem not to have immediate relevance. A consequence of this in psychological terms is that we can become locked into a limited perception of the nature of the danger, and of the range of possible response strategies. The feeling that 'there is nothing I can do, this is all beyond my competence', may be more a reflection of this rigid locking than of my real capacity to respond. As one who dabbled in his youth in rock climbing, I have vivid memories of experiencing that feeling of being frozen, incapable of forward or backward movement; safest just to stay still! So it can be in life: danger can produce a 'freeze' reaction, and that can become ingrained. The consequence of this in our attempts to face the challenges that life throws at us is that our response can be characterized by inappropriate rigidity. The purpose of the second phase of counselling, then, is that the client be helped to loosen the constraining, uni-dimensional perspectives that reduce or remove her or his capacity for action. The actual techniques available to the counsellor are described in Chapter 8, but it is useful at this point to bear in mind the centrality of the quality of the relationship. That relationship must produce a profound feeling of safety and trust in the client if movement is to occur. As I froze against a rock face, it was no use for people to yell advice from above or below about what to do. What I needed was a trusted leader, who could climb down to my level, not pushing or pressuring, simply staying with me and helping me to see possibilities other than staying locked on to Crag Lough for all eternity. So it is in the second phase of counselling. It is enormously challenging to face and tackle issues where I am locked and frozen; as Egan says, the counsellor earns the right to challenge by communicating the intense commitment and safety which characterize the counselling relationship. Eventually, I will find myself seeing new courses of action, other, previously inconceivable possibilities, and I may with my counsellor find myself saying, 'Yes, I see that I can move, and I want to make *this* particular move, but I don't know how.' And so to the third phase, that of action.

ACTION

By now the client has made a considerable journey of exploration, initially superficial and then at greater depth, marked by two key points: the confident identification of the challenge to be faced ('this is what is really getting me down') and the slow, resolute, sometimes fearful generation of a new way of looking at the possible responses, which allows the client to say, 'this is what I want to do'. The specific techniques for helping forward movement in action will be explored in Chapter 8, but it is appropriate to indicate that the client will need help to choose a specific course of action which she or he finds desirable and feasible, some help in implementing that desired action, further support in evaluating the extent of its success and a refinement of the plan if necessary. Our map now includes not only an overview of the kind of relationship within which counselling occurs, but also an appreciation of the process (see Figure 4.1) which the client will follow and which the counsellor must facilitate (see Figure 4.2), using the skills and techniques to be explored in detail later.

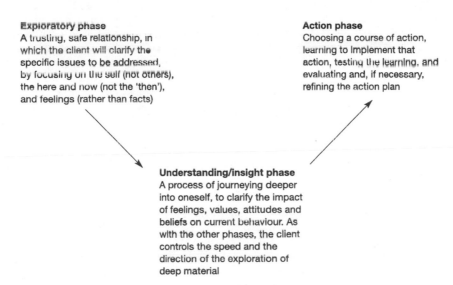

Exploratory phase
A trusting, safe relationship, in which the client will clarify the specific issues to be addressed, by focusing on the self (not others), the here and now (not the 'then'), and feelings (rather than facts)

Action phase
Choosing a course of action, learning to implement that action, testing the learning, and evaluating and, if necessary, refining the action plan

Understanding/insight phase
A process of journeying deeper into oneself, to clarify the impact of feelings, values, attitudes and beliefs on current behaviour. As with the other phases, the client controls the speed and the direction of the exploration of deep material

Figure 4.1 The tri-phasic process of counselling (the client)

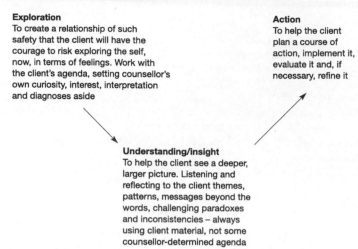

Exploration
To create a relationship of such safety that the client will have the courage to risk exploring the self, now, in terms of feelings. Work with the client's agenda, setting counsellor's own curiosity, interest, interpretation and diagnoses aside

Action
To help the client plan a course of action, implement it, evaluate it and, if necessary, refine it

Understanding/insight
To help the client see a deeper, larger picture. Listening and reflecting to the client themes, patterns, messages beyond the words, challenging paradoxes and inconsistencies – always using client material, not some counsellor-determined agenda

Figure 4.2 The tri-phasic process of counselling (the counsellor)

This is the challenge for the client, and the requirement on the counsellor is to make a response to such a challenge possible. Thus, for each phase of counselling the counsellor needs, within a relationship infused by the core conditions, to be able to balance support and challenge for the client in such a way that the client will feel safe enough to explore honestly, to let go of the false security offered in the locked, rigid perceptions adopted, and to reach out, risk-taking, to new coping behaviours.

We can close this section by reflecting on the contrast between the real demands made of the counsellor, and more traditional, teacher-centred attempts to help. Egan (1986) identifies a number of common errors counsellors make in the initial phase of counselling – they are characteristic of the problem-solving, 'let's get this sorted quickly' approach that all of us are tempted to use when in a hurry. Our responses can be judgemental, evaluative, based on *my* agenda and experience. They can offer completely inappropriate reassurance, thereby rejecting the real feelings of the client. I can be lofty, condescending, manipulative, with the 'good' of the pupil as my objective. Suggestions for action, advice, 'if I were you', taking over the autonomy of the client, also block progress. I can feel frustrated that the student is not listening to me, and express that with exasperation and lack of respect. In a word, I can fail genuinely to work on the client's agenda, reshaping it to something closer to my own experience, and to something I am more comfortable with. As always, Rogers's challenge is there. Our message to the client is 'Is this where you are? Am I with you? Is this the direction in which you are headed?'

So, counselling as an activity begins to take shape. We now know it to be centrally a special kind of relationship, with observable characteristics that all of us have to some extent, and which can be developed to high, very facilitative levels. We know, too, that it is a process, a movement in the client from, in some sense, maladaptiveness to greater degree of adaptiveness. The third component of the activity is a vast complex of skills and techniques, some of which at first glance seem straightforward and unproblematic, but all of which merit very careful scrutiny.

COUNSELLING: THE SKILLS AND TECHNIQUES

When Eysenck (1953) spoke of the 'talking cure', he was speaking of a therapy in which words were to be central. He could also have called it the 'listening cure', since from the counsellor's point of view a key skill is the fundamental ability to listen to the words and other communication the client shares. It is regarded as a compliment if we say of someone, 'she is a good listener'; to be truly attended to, listened to, is an enabling, affirming experience. No less, to be ignored, for someone to walk out when we are speaking, to see someone yawning or looking at a watch as we share, for us, fascinating experiences, is totally devaluing. We begin to perceive ourselves as without merit, unworthy of attention. To be listened to creates the obverse reaction: we become central, not peripheral, worthy of attention, not encumbrances to be discarded. So how good a listener am I? Many of us will remember the period in our children's development when they don't stop talking: silly jokes, stories which leave absolutely nothing out, challenges; and of course the questions. Most of us develop a capacity to drop into automatic pilot – 'Mmm . . . how lovely . . . really? . . . That must have been nice' – but very frequently we get caught out. People seem to sense when they are genuinely the object of attention. I recall one of my own children, about 7 years old, suddenly realizing that we were on 'automatic'. She was indignant, and began her reproach, with no change of tone or posture, but the anger was there. She told us of it years later: 'And then Mrs Bullen made us all stand in a line, next to the wall with cracks in it, you know, the one where my picture of grandad used to be when we had the Christmas play. Julie was Mary, and Billy was a shepherd and wee-ed himself.' Parental response ran something like this: 'Did she really, oh dear, mmm . . . mm, yes, *love*' (what a con to stick that in!). Then the child, realizing that she was not being listened to, takes her revenge: 'So, I'm going upstairs now to open the window (really, how lovely), and I'm going to climb out on to the verandah (yes, love), and I'm going to jump into the garden (that's great), on to the rockery (don't hurt yourself love), and die (oh, that's lovely). *You're not listening!*' 'Of course I am, I always listen to you.'

Do I? Really listen? It is the basic skill of the counsellor, and we need to test our listening skills, critically analyse them and refine them. Beyond the deliberate escape from unwanted verbal assaults of all kinds, Gordon (1974) offers a challenging list of things that we tend to do when we claim to be listening. He suggests that we keep dropping our listening mode to move internally, while still nodding or holding eye contact to simulate an attention we are not giving, into such extraneous activities as judgement, evaluation, comparison, preparing a question, moralizing, problem-solving, data preparation and so on. Having dropped out of listening, even momentarily, we are missing the client agenda. The good listener doesn't miss things, the mediocre listener fills in the gaps with interpretation, speculation, her or his own material. That is why a fifty-minute counselling session is so tiring – the discipline of really listening requires enormous psychological and physical energy. So, what is the skill?

The skill is to be able to focus fully on the communication of the client, without any of the distractions indicated by Gordon. We check the accuracy of the listening by asking the speaker. It is the source of many jokes about counselling: that counsellors simply repeat the words of the client, in an ever-decreasing circle that has them both disappearing into the void. But the sheer power of having our own words accurately reflected to us is difficult to imagine: it challenges us to reflect on the accuracy of the throwaway remark, it gives us access to material that has for years hovered on the threshold of the conscious, it invites us to recast material in a way that on reflection seems to fit our view better, it demands commitment from the speaker to what she or he is saying, or a rephrasing, or a retraction.

A pupil with homework problems cites a crowded house and the demands of an elderly relative as blocks on his work. The openness of the student is not accidental. He feels he is in a safe enough relationship to disclose deep feelings.

> *Client*: I can't stick her. I think old people ought to be in a home. I hate them.
> *Counsellor*: So, you're saying that you can't stand your granny and you so hate the elderly that you think they ought to be put in homes just for them.
> *Client*: Well, I don't hate all of them. But my gran really gets up my nose.
> *Counsellor*: It's not that you hate them, that feels too strong a word for you. But your gran annoys you so much, that sometimes it feels like hate?
> *Client*: Yeah, you've no idea the things she does.
> *Counsellor*: No, you're right, I don't.

What does a granny do to generate such a reaction? Note that the counsellor is listening, reflecting, asking 'Is this where you are, where you want to be?', not allowing curiosity and his agenda to intrude with a 'But what on earth does she do?' An off-the-cuff expression of 'hatred' is immediately withdrawn when it is given back to the client. Without any intrusive questions the counsellor has helped the client to arrive at the point where details of the grandchild–grandparent interaction seem natural. There is no judgement ('Oh, come on Joe, you don't really hate them') or moralizing ('Have you thought, Joe that we all get old sometime, even you?') or problem-solving ('Perhaps you could just keep out of her way'), there is the expression of empathy and unconditional positive regard provided by the client-centred listener. With that, little by little, Joe will arrive at his own response to the challenge of granny.

The listening described above is quite near the surface. In the literature (Egan, 1986) it is described as *primary-level empathy*, i.e. the skill of listening meticulously, hearing accurately, reflecting with great precision the material (facts, behaviours, feelings, values) that the client presents in verbal disclosures. For the counsellor, there are also disclosures which lie 'beyond the words', and an ability to listen meticulously at that level, to hear accurately, to reflect with precision, but more tentatively, the disclosures that are made in many non-verbal modes is an extension of the skill of listening. Again, it indicates to the client that she or he is worthy of the kind of close attention that is suggested by counsellor sensitivity to the whole, communicating client. A client who was highly intelligent, a coper, but deeply wounded, illustrates this type of listening, which is called *advanced-level empathy*. At a verbal level the client was very skilled at presenting herself as 'OK', but her work and occasional outbursts of verbal aggression suggested that there was something causing trouble. She came for counselling, half of her wanting to get rid of the internal tensions of which she was vaguely aware, and half of her wanting to cling on to the coping strategies she had elaborated over the years. The counsellor listened. She told her story: facts about family, events, physical abuse, the death of her mother; feelings about being no good, a burden, about the death of a protective mother, and ambivalence towards a violent but sometimes affectionate father; about her tendency to explode, kick over the traces. 'But really, I'm OK; it's just that sometimes it all gets on top of me.'

Counsellor: All?
Client: Yes, everything that's happened. [Pause. The client tentatively approaches the source of her pain. She knows deep down that she has locked it away to protect herself, and almost inaudibly adds] Especially mum.
Counsellor: There's a lot of pain there.
Client: [sighs, nods] Mmhmm. But I'm OK, really. [This is close to deep, painful material; perhaps for the counsellor, too. Will she or he really listen beyond the words?]
Counsellor: I can hear a very strong person saying, 'I'm OK, really', and I also sense a very vulnerable one, telling me 'I'm hurting'. [The counsellor had listened to the slight break in the voice, the misting of the eyes, and reflected it back to the client. Note too the more tentative nature of advanced empathy – it tries to respond to the client's agenda in the same way as with words, but the counsellor says, 'and I also *sense* . . .' in recognition of the greater difficulty of listening accurately 'beyond the words'.]

We will look in more detail at working with deep material in Chapter 6, but for the moment suffice it to say that right through the process of counselling, we work with our client's material. We do not interpret; we listen, reflect, give back to the client the material that is being painfully generated. Sometimes our reflections will be of the client's lengthy silences: 'you don't know where to start' or 'everything seems to be a mass of confusion' or, if the client is evidently distraught (tears, hanky twisting), 'there is a well of tears/sadness'. These lines are not presented as recipes to be followed, but rather as indicators of the kind of material from the client that merits our response, and examples of kinds of response that material might elicit. Nor, even here in working with client silence, are we putting in our agenda, or interpreting. We are listening, and in this case listening beyond the words, to that complex repertoire of non-verbal communicators humans use.

   In addition to listening, counsellors also need to develop the ability to paraphrase or summarize a substantial piece of disclosure. Not all clients are silent; some are very verbal, and we need to be able to help them in structuring, ordering, prioritizing large chunks of material. Again, this will lead us to be tentative, so that we do not offer a priority of what seems to us to be most significant. Rather we facilitate their work of structuring: 'You've talked a lot about your sister, and the times when her boyfriend is staying at your house. You mentioned that your mum seems to forget you exist, when your sister comes home. And you told me about your own boyfriend, and the problems your dad creates because he thinks you're too young to have a steady boyfriend. That's a lot of challenges; I'm not sure whether you see any one of them as the chief issue, the one you'd like to get your teeth into now.' Coleman's (1980) focal theory of adolescence explains why some young people collapse under the strain of growing up and others cope quite effectively. He suggests it is the arrival of several challenges together (e.g. peer relationships, relationships with the opposite sex, parents, work and independence, perhaps some traumatic event), and the resultant confusion about which way to turn, that tips the balance. What is really bothering this client?' Only she knows, and she needs lots of space to search and decide.

A further set of skills the counsellor deploys involves the ability to give back to the client patterns, themes and consistently repeated issues.

> *Client*: We always go to the same place for our holidays. When I was little, I used to like it, all the games on the beach, all together; but I'm past that now; I want to be on my own more. I just want to be me, in my own way.
> *Counsellor*: You've talked about your independence a lot; that seems to be a very important thing for you.
> *Client*: It's everything.

But the counsellor also needs to be sensitive to, and pick up, inconsistencies, possibly unconscious, in the disclosures of the client.

> *Counsellor*: You say it's everything, and I can see that your independence is very close to your heart. I'm not quite sure how, when you say that with such force, it fits in with something you said before. Something on the lines that 'I really love my family, especially my mum'.

The counsellor challenges, but doesn't contradict, argue, attack discrepancy as illogical. She or he understands the assertion of Brammer and Shostrum (1982) that one of the outcomes of counselling is the growing ability of the client to accept and live with ambiguity, and that, in order to help the client do that, the skill of supportive, client-centred challenge is necessary. It is an invitation for the client to face the inconsistency, not a confrontation.

Thus the two fundamental skills of the counsellor (and of the teacher) are the abilities to *support* the client – creating the ambience of safety which will encourage creative risk-taking and courageous exploration – and to *challenge* the client, having won the right to do that by establishing the initial relationship of trust. Premature challenge can be perceived by the client as attack, and the normal response to that is closure and defence. In subsequent chapters, as we move more into the activity of counselling, other techniques will be explored. We now have not only an overview of counselling, but a detailed analysis of its key elements.

This then is counselling: a relationship of such quality that clients are encouraged to take exploratory and decision-making risks involved in change, supported and aided by the skill and techniques of the counsellor. How might it be of use to the teacher? The next chapter will take us into some case material to illustrate how both the classroom teacher and the specialist school counsellor might proceed.

Exercises

Learning to listen is a central activity for a counsellor or teacher. If we are to start at the right point, tackle the right issues, we need to go to where the learner is, and if we do not listen, we will not know where she or he is. For both the counsellor and the teacher, listening respectfully, accepting the learner's agenda instead of imposing ours, is a major statement of the value we see in that person. It is not only about accruing information and returning it accurately to the client, it is an important way of signalling unconditional positive regard, empathy, genuineness and immediacy, the core conditions for effective counselling. Being listened to is an experience with deep emotional implications. We will try in these exercises to explore some of them.

Being not listened to

Working in pairs, take it in turns to be listener and listened to. The task here for the listener is not to listen, in an obvious way. The client is invited to 'take three minutes to tell your partner of an enjoyable experience during your last holidays'. The listener can turn away, yawn, look at his or her watch, file nails, etc., signalling little interest and minimal listening. After each person has had a turn, talk about how it felt to be ignored (even though you both knew it was an exercise), and what impact it had on your telling the 'enjoyable experience' story. Think carefully about the experience.

Participants often speak of being annoyed or belittled, even in an exercise. The savour of what had been an enjoyable experience is taken away or diminished, and there can be a tendency to stop talking: what's the point, you're not listening? Some useful insights can be generated into the implications for teaching and counselling from this brief experience of not being listened to.

Being listened to: facts

Working in the same pairs, you have a similar task, but this time your listening skills will be really deployed; you will not be sabotaging. In turns, the 'client' is asked to spend three minutes on an experience involving response to an emergency. Listen carefully, and then, in as much detail as possible, respond to your partner in the form 'You have just told me that . . .' Then change roles. What do you notice about listening? Did you find yourself doing anything else, as well as trying to listen? Were you able to retain the information revealed in the three-minute session? Did you remember selectively? What was the (unconscious?) criterion for selection? Did you find yourself tempted to, or did you, do more than 'reflect back' to your client; for example, make suggestions or use your expertise? As a client, what was your perception?

Did you feel listened to? Can you describe the feeling? What signs made it clear to you? Did you feel you lost the attention of your listener at all in the three minutes? What suggested that to you? Can you describe how you felt?

Again, the actual experience and analysis of the experience of being listened to can give us insight into the challenge of what seems to be an everyday issue. Participants will often comment on how tiring it is to 'really listen', even though it is only for three minutes. The temptation to take a sly break in a longer session can lead us to miss important disclosures – and clients do notice, and register the lowering of respect, attention and empathy. Memory is mentioned, too: the difficulty of picking up and retaining everything. It is consoling to note that clients will return to important material if for some reason the counsellor fails to respond to it. An incident like the one in the exercise can also have us, instead of listening, making our own internal responses to the 'emergency' – we drop into comparing, judging, evaluating instead of listening.

Being listened to: the feelings

Since our feelings, values, emotions and attitudes reside deeper in our self than do our cognitive material and our logical responses to challenge, they tend to be more protected, less easily shared and needy of a great sense of safety if they are to be disclosed. Judgemental responses and criticism can push them back deep into the persona, making them much less willing to emerge. The material of this exercise deliberately focuses on pleasant feelings; to look at unpleasant feelings is much more challenging. Nevertheless, it is still possible to get a hint of the intimacy, the 'me'-ness of feelings.

Still in pairs, I would like to suggest another listening exercise, with a slightly different focus – feelings. As always, each person is free to participate or not. Taking it in turns as before, can each of you spend three minutes sharing with your listener a statement about your favourite room or place. Choose somewhere that makes you feel comfortable, safe and at peace. The listener's task is as before, to listen as carefully as possible. When the sharing is finished, the listener has a slightly different task. Instead of reflecting back in the 'You told me . . .' form, try to be your client, by using the 'I' form, as if you were the original speaker, getting as close as possible to what you heard from your partner: 'I have this beautiful room that overlooks the river . . .' When both have had a turn as speaker and listener, process the experience from both perspectives. Do you note any difference in disclosing feelings rather than facts, behaviours or events? Can you put your finger on the differences? As a listener, what differences do you note? Did you listen, or were you thinking, 'Oh, yes, I would like that . . .' or 'Good heavens, that's just like mine . . . ' or 'What a good idea, I could put mine like that . . . ' The temptation to cease listening and to evaluate is always strong, and when we give in to the temptation, it usually shows in the quality of our reflection. Was I able to empathize with the speaker's feelings about the special place? Did I catch any feelings, or was it only physical description that I heard: 'A beautiful pale beige carpet with two deep brown sofas and an open fire'? On reflection now, can you find three words each to describe any feelings you detected in the encounters? If these words were not said, what communication puts them into your mind now: your partner's body language, tone of voice? Do you listen beyond the words? Is it unconscious, or are you aware of doing it?

The exercises in the next chapter will look in more detail at the listening skills involved in 'advanced-level empathy' and immediacy, but we can conclude this chapter by trying an exercise which challenges our listening skills and our ability to work with our client's agenda, not our own expertise, problem-solving skills, curiosity or interests. What is the client saying, communicating? Am I sure? Can I check it out with accurate, non-judgemental reflection?

Being listened to: serial counselling

It is possible to draw a line representing human communication, which runs from brainwashing, browbeating, through interrogating and cross-examining, past questioning, problem-solving and informing, to reassuring and calming. It is easy to note the direction of the line, from nil concern for the object of our attention to great concern and care. It may be of interest to try to situate teaching on the continuum, perhaps noting that it is a complex and variable form of communicating, changing according to circumstances. (Am I 'brainwashing' when my 3-year-old, each time he tries to poke scissors into an electric power point, is told 'no'?) However, one feature of the continuum we might fail to note is that the whole of it is controlled by the other person: from the brainwasher to the calmer, the control lies with the other. The consistent claim of Rogers is that for counselling to occur, we need to pass the control to the client. He goes further in his 1983 text by making the same claim about teaching. If the claim is true, then we need to extend the continuum, beyond reassuring and calming to a challenging style of facilitating, liberating and enabling. To do this we need to work only with the client's agenda.

> We need a volunteer to be a client. So that you know what you are letting yourself in for, I'll run through what we're going to do. The volunteer will be asked to start this listening exercise by saying, 'I'd like to tell you about something I've always wanted to do, but so far have never managed.' The whole group is sitting in a circle, including the client. As soon as the client has presented his or her initial statement, the 'counselling session' begins. In a clockwise direction, in turn, starting with the person on the client's left, each participant has one intervention. The task is to listen meticulously and reflect accurately. Since each of us has only one intervention, we cannot 'follow a line of enquiry'; there is a discipline to listen and reflect. Thus the first person might say, 'I notice that you said, "so far . . . "' The client might respond, 'Well, I haven't given up hope, yet.' The second 'counsellor' may reflect, 'I hear the enthusiasm in your voice when you talk about your wish, and the optimism of the "so far", but the "haven't given up, yet", that "yet" sounds a bit desperate . . . ' and so on. The temptations to say, 'Why

*don't you . . . or 'Have you thought about . . . ' will be there, but they
are our agenda – as Rogers says, we must go with the wisdom of the
client.*

After all have participated, perhaps with two rounds, a discussion of the exercise
will reveal a great deal of material about agendas, control, facilitation and the
challenge to the client to explore her or his material, not the material of the
counsellor. Can I subordinate my interests and competencies to the client's own
material, much of which may be buried?

In McGuiness (1989, pp. 108–9), the following account describes one outcome
of this exercise, carried out early in a training course. Note how the counsellor
agenda, not the client agenda, dominates, and the consequence:

> *Client*: Well . . . it's not very much, really . . . I suppose I'd like to talk
> about the birth of my first child.
> *Response 1*: Were you present at the birth? [Counsellor curiosity,
> counsellor agenda, warm, interested, but *not* counselling.]
> *Client*: No, in those days we didn't do that sort of thing.
> *Response 2*: Was it a long labour? [From a female colleague. Again, her
> agenda, empathizing with the mother's possible, imagined challenge. We
> are counselling the father.]
> *Client*: I'm not sure what counts as long; it was about eight hours
> altogether.
> *Response 3*: Was the baby born in hospital? [It was possible to sense in
> the group some desperate attempt to elicit information. Why is this guy
> telling us this? It was just a listening exercise, but we had this urge to
> shape it, give it our meaning.]
> *Client*: Yes.
> *Response 4*: Was it a boy or a girl? [Of interest to us, but perhaps totally
> insignificant for the client. Listening has stopped; we are off on a mystery
> tour of our – composite – agenda. Unable to follow a line, we are
> confused, searching, trying to establish a pattern, when our task is to
> facilitate the client's exploration.]

After questions that made my eyes water from mothers in the group, the eighth
response came – pure reflective listening, totally on the client's agenda, so
facilitative. 'I was puzzled that you said the birth of your first child wasn't very
much really; I think that was the phrase.' The client paused; we could see him
processing his own words, his agenda. Then, 'Yes, you're right. I did say that. I
suppose I said it because the baby died.' None of the questions, our agenda,
elicited that piece of information, but the one person who stayed with the client
agenda made it possible for him to share it; and no doubt communicated to him
just how carefully she was listening to him.

CHAPTER 5

Cries for help: counselling in schools

I would like for a moment to refer back to the moving hymn to the humanity of young people quoted from Pablo Casals at the opening of the second chapter. He contrasts our obsession with factual knowledge and our failure to perceive the uniqueness of children. He reminds us of a different educational agenda, one that starts from a set of assumptions notably at variance with the ones that currently underpin education policy. No doubt, for some, a cry for help that *ought* to be heard from the classroom is: 'Help, I do not know . . . that Paris is the capital of France.' Casals presses us to reflect that perhaps other cries need our attention first: 'Help, I lack a sense of worth; help, I feel I am without value; help, I have no one to turn to.' I recently asked a professional geographer for an answer to a factual question that my geography O level had not given me. He did not know the answer, though of course he knew how to find out. What is the capital of Rwanda? We discovered it to be Kigali. How about Burundi? Again, my specialist friend did not know: 'But why do you want to know?' he queries. For the same reason I want pupils to know that Paris is the capital of France, I thought, but said, 'To make a point about the transitory nature of information.' I do not know for certain, but I suspect that neither Burundi nor Rwanda existed when I did my O level, and that if they did, they had names that politics and time have changed. I do not feel that I need to cry for help, not knowing, and am aware that there must be many new countries whose capitals I do not know. But there are other things that I would have liked to have had help with at school – mostly things to do with the confusion of growing up. Murgatroyd and Woolf (1982) suggested a list of 'potential stressors' faced by adolescents. Even now, I recall experiencing almost all of them; and I remember receiving very little help to cope. Adolescents will bring to the classroom:

- a feeling that they are falling short of standards and expectations;
- an uncertainty or fear about future choices;
- a feeling of being fragmented, not a whole person, not knowing what to do;
- a feeling of dependence and simultaneously a desire to be autonomous;
- being unwilling to set limits, yet knowing they must be set;
- uncertainty about employment, adulthood;
- uncertainty about sex roles;

- difficulty in making and sustaining significant relationships;
- feeling overwhelmed by the range of emotions that emerge out of consciousness;
- problems in accepting responsibility (being over- or under-responsive).

I was one of the 'clever' ones, Cambridge-bound, and in some senses a success. The fact that my wife can sometimes claim that my adolescence continued until I was 30 suggests that the success was limited. The cries for help are very muted, but they are there.

Curious about the capital of Burundi? Good; that's a useful lesson to have learned, to be curious. Don't give a damn? Now, where did I learn *that* attitude to information? I do not want to over-press the Casals position, since there are of course information bases that we need in order to negotiate our world. But what I would like to press is the idea that as teachers we need to have our critical faculties sharpened to exquisite acuity as we evaluate the curricular demands made of our young people. Any curriculum is a complex statement about the values of those proposing it. It has implications about social, emotional, moral and political priorities, and about the nature of education. It is one navigation point (one of several) for our pupils; it contributes to their attempts to answer the challenges cited above.

Take a class of 30 pupils in Year 9, 14- and 15-year-olds. I have them next for French. I know it will be a good class: I'm feeling good, enthusiastic; I've prepared well – some solid grammar, a good game to catch their attention, some conversational work in pairs, a small written piece and a bouncy closure. Yes, this is one of my goodies. I look out of the staffroom window and see a few of them in the playground: earnest conversations in nooks and crannies, boisterous careering about, borderline inconsiderate behaviour elsewhere, some isolation, deep friendships; growing up, learning, as Casals demanded, that they 'are a marvel . . . are unique', that 'in the millions of years that have passed, there has never been another child like you'. I hope I can bear that in mind as we wrestle in ten minutes with the perfect tense. I have eighteen girls and twelve boys, and I know the statistics of a random sample of teenagers and their experiences. The group will include victims of sexual abuse, physical abuse, emotional abuse; there will be individuals who bully and their victims; there will be children who have been bereaved; sometimes members of the group will have suffered the trauma of seeing or experiencing violence; there may be pupils with special intellectual needs or enduring physical illness; and all of them will be coping to one degree or another with the challenge of being on the threshold of being adult. I wonder if they know the capital of Burundi?

It is too easy to become a Jeremiah, to exaggerate the problematic – these young people are growing up, a natural process. There is a danger that we might become the psychological equivalent of ambulance chasers – always on the lookout for injury, accidents and illness, seeing problems where there are none. That is clearly not my suggestion. However, an obverse error would be to presume that all the young people in our school are fine, and do not need developmental help to cope with the normal challenges of adolescence, or the special responses sometimes necessary to emerge whole from specific traumas. What we need is not an intrusive, problem-ferreting, nosey, dominant approach, but a climate in which cries for help are permitted and there is a systematic sensitivity to any cries for help that might be made, both as an organization and at the level of individual teachers. To pick up the messages we need a mental set and highly tuned antennae that accept that they exist.

Much has been written (Best *et al.*, 1977, 1983; Lang, 1988; McGuiness, 1989; National Association for Pastoral Care in Education (NAPCE), *passim*) on the pastoral care systems of our schools, the formal, organizational response to both the development of pupils as persons and their less frequent, but no less real, problems. I do not propose to try to summarize that material, but direct readers to the NAPCE journal, *Pastoral Care in Education*, which supplies a constant stream of practitioner-focused material on pastoral care. While recognizing that the vast majority of schools have tutorial systems, heads of year with oversight of sections of the school, periods of personal and social education (PSE) and so on, I would like to focus our attention on the micro-issues of the individual subject teacher's sensitivity to cries for help. If it is really the case that in my fictional class of modern language students there is a constant presence of children with major problems, I can either avert my gaze or try to respond to their needs. Fundamentally there are two phenomena. First, the messages of help are sent out: what are they, how are they sent, what kind of things do they say? Second, the antennae which we project into the school pick up those messages. We can look at four different areas of activity of the students: their work, behaviour, peer relationships and relationships with adults; their health, too, can be a powerful indicator that all is not well. Alongside the areas in which adolescents communicate, we can look for three types of messages that are sent out: things the young people do, things they don't do and things they say or don't say and their body language.

Teachers have available to them a range of normed instruments which offer a structured analysis of the areas identified above: the Lewis Counselling Inventory (NFER, 1980) and the Bristol Social Adjustment Guide (BSAG), constructed by D.H. Stott (1976), are two of the more accessible ones for teachers. Many of the tests are available only to those trained in their use, so the classroom teacher would not have access to many on publishers' current lists. The National Foundation for Educational Research (NFER) has a detailed qualification system, and those wanting to explore the potential of tests, and their own level of qualification as testers, will receive detailed information by writing to it (see appendix for address). While I recognize the occasional need for and usefulness of testing in counselling situations, I am fully convinced by the arguments assembled by Nelson-Jones (1982), that the use of 'saturation testing' (i.e. group administration of a battery of tests) is the result of administrative imperatives, 'where there is insufficient *counselling* time to discover individual testing needs', not a demonstration to the subjects of their 'inviolable worth'. The ethos of testing *can* run counter to the communication of the core conditions. It should not have that effect, and Cronbach's (1970) text gives detail on how testing ought to take place. However, when the BSAG manual claims that the test offers 'a quick means by which . . . counsellors can keep themselves informed of children's adjustment' (p. 7), I am left wondering whether what we really need is something that is not so quick and has a more individualized feel to it.

That something is the core condition of 'immediacy'. In counselling terms, immediacy involves a highly developed sense of awareness of the dynamics in a relationship. Thus it requires the counsellor to be 'in tune' with her or his own feelings, emotions and sensations during a working session (Tudor and Worrall, 1994). Further, the counsellor needs to be able to 'be and live' those elements, and to be willing to communicate that awareness to the client, within an ethical framework which coherently assesses the appropriateness of doing so. Such awareness, and the willingness to communicate it, makes the relationship with the client 'genuine'. No psychological energy is wasted in maintaining pretence, facade, defence. It is the contrary of the denial of experiences. It makes a relationship 'clean'.

I remember a day conference I was to run (careers counselling, as I recall) at a college other than my own. Delegates, travelling long distances, had left home before first light on a gloomy November morning, to arrive promptly for a 9.00 a.m. start. I was at the college at 8.15 to set up the room. No porters arrived until 8.40. Several long-distance travellers had arrived expecting coffee. They seemed justifiably annoyed. The porters had keys, but no information on the conference. I showed the letter of confirmation, with room booking, date, time, meals and the signature of a (still absent) conference officer. Nine o'clock and the delinquent arrived. I saw his face fall, as the porter dashed out to meet him and ask him what was going on. 'Oh, God. What can I say? I'm terribly sorry. It's on my desk – last thing before I went home. I must have forgotten.' By now it was 9.30, coffee finally arrived and the conference got under way, almost an hour late. I had tried to explain to the group, and to apologize, but I did not have to be a Carl Rogers to detect that they were very angry. Intent on getting the relationship 'clean' from the beginning, I decided to start with a quick exercise in which everyone (fifteen of us) was invited to complete the phrase, 'At this moment I am feeling . . .', with the instruction that we might want to express any negative feelings that were still around and possibly get in the way of our work.

One by one, using slightly different phrases, the denials came: 'I'm fine; I was a bit annoyed, but these things happen, and I'm OK'; 'No comment, I don't get rattled by things that can't be helped'; 'Let's not waste any more time, and get on with it'; 'What's done is done; you've apologized, the college has apologized. It's time to work.' And so on. No one took up the actual invitation, 'At this moment I am feeling . . . ' They went to their heads, their sense of responsibility, their innate courtesy, some vision of social, professional behaviour. Nothing of their emotions, visceral experiences, sensations, which though denied were still there, and about to impinge on the day. My own contribution had been to say, 'At this moment I feel angry with the college, I feel let down and I have stress ache in my stomach. I somehow want to make the day worth it for you.' We began work, and I spent the most difficult training morning of my life. The group was lethargic, truculent, uncooperative, bordered on the aggressive, to such an extent that I left the group members to their lunch while I found a quiet spot to think out what was going on. I decided that we had found ourselves in an inauthentic, counterproductive, dishonest relationship, in which our potential for learning was being subverted by a deeper, unexpressed agenda. We were pretending to work on careers education, when in reality we were still working through the first experiences of the day. The hidden agenda needed to be addressed, and the way to do it was by being immediate, congruent, genuine.

Nelson-Jones (1982) speaks of immediacy thus: 'frequently people have in their relationships tacit agreements not to notice or talk about certain areas of the relationship. Immediacy relates to the capacity of people to respond immediately to their experiencing of a relationship, and to disclose what might otherwise be left unsaid' (p. 344). It is a very powerful form of relating and is only effective if it occurs within a relationship of deep trust. The challenging of denial, the confronting of pretence, can have the effect of crushing exploration if it is not accompanied by a communication of unconditional positive regard. My decision in the conference was to start the afternoon session by talking about immediacy and the effect it can have on a (teaching) relationship and by communicating my own immediacy, which was that we were still working on subconscious issues. I invited the group to do again the exercise of the morning session: 'At this moment, I am feeling . . . ' The result was entirely different. Lunch, my mini-presentation on the nature of immediacy or some god of counselling led the group to such comments as, 'At this moment I am feeling ashamed that I chickened out of the exercise this morning', or 'I am feeling at this moment freed from the pretending that, for some reason, I engaged in this morning', or 'At this moment, I feel a residual resentment about the late start this morning, and also pleased that we are actually talking honestly as a group, as counsellors should' and so on. The atmosphere of the group changed dramatically, and in the short time we had left to us we worked like Trojans.

Immediacy in a relationship is challenging. It can suggest an intrusive, controlling scrutiny of the subject, or, as should be the case, a supportive, warm, unconditional regarding of that client that leaves me so close that I am almost experiencing things that she or he is experiencing. It requires me first of all to be aware of myself – the 'now' of existence, so much of it unconsidered, transitory, beyond reach, yet all of it powering into my relationships. And it makes me choose, ethically, to disclose those elements of my awareness which seem crucial to the relationship, not self-indulgently, but in a client-centred way. The exercises at the end of the chapter will suggest ways of exploring how to develop some of the skills related to this important part of the counselling relationship.

The bell has gone, and my French group wander, with varying degrees of enthusiasm, into the language room. Immediacy, I chant to myself. What am I aware of *now*? Despite all the careful preparation, I am anxious that it might not go well. I am aware that one of my car tyres is bald, and I must get it changed; and that I really like most of these kids and want them to do well. My back is aching just below the right scapula. Cirrhosis? Cancer? I am really looking forward to *La Traviata* tonight . . . What a complex creature I am. Can I really learn to 'be' that complex me, with all its ambiguity, or will I settle for a public persona, denying, repressing the rest? It feels good not to deny; almost a liberation. What can I, do I, ethically, disclose? What a professional question!

And the pupils. What does my skill in immediacy allow me to receive from them? Surely it is easier to let them pass through: stereotypical faces, images, little contact, no relationship. Who in this group is coming to learn French having shared a bed with a younger sibling who pee-ed on her in the small hours? The discomfort, the shame still there. Is there someone here whose grandmother died at the weekend, or who is still working through the grief of losing a parent or a brother or sister? Is someone's sexuality being destroyed in an exploitative relationship, or is someone learning day after day that he is worthless? Would I notice?

The individuals in my French class could in theory *tell* me that they are in pain, they could cry 'help', but few will do so in an obvious way. They are not sure how we will react, so they check us out. Figure 5.1 may help to structure the experience of the classroom. It is not intended as a 'test' or instrument in a formal sense, but it may serve as an *aide-mémoire*.

There's Tom. I'm not his tutor, but our pastoral system is good on communication and I know that his dad has recently been made redundant. I have noticed that Tom is less chatty, more thoughtful. He is getting on with his work better. He seems to have grown up rather quickly. When the redundancies occurred, to say 'sorry to hear about your dad's job' may have seemed pointless, but it was what I felt. I have never been made redundant – my children have not yet had to face belt-tightening at home – but I can sense that it puts French into a different perspective. I need to communicate to Tom something of the empathy, the continuing regard, my own reactions, by listening to all the messages (Figure 5.1) he is giving me. Nor should I overwhelm him; it is the unobtrusive maintenance of Egan's (1993) 'culture of vigilance'.

	Work	Behaviour	Relationships with peers	Relationships with adults	Health
Things said					
Things not said					
Things done					
Things not done					
Non-verbal communication					

Figure 5.1 Cries for help

Betty is a different matter. Where Tom sends out messages that he is facing and responding to a major family crisis, Betty's pain is almost palpable. I have no idea what is bothering her, nor does her tutor. We are watching carefully, not intruding, interpreting – trying to help her feel safe in a way that may give her the confidence to say 'help'. At the moment, our job is to communicate the core conditions of unconditional positive regard, empathy, genuineness and immediacy – the elements that Rogers claims facilitate therapeutic movement. Betty arrived at the school in September, from a school and town 180 miles to the south of us. Her mother, an immaculate, slightly anxious and eager-to-please woman, accompanies her daughter and tells the year head that she 'has always been very quiet; in her own little world, aren't you love'. We have a transfer file from the original school – Betty is of above average intelligence, underachieving, socially an isolate, extremely reticent. The same characteristics continued in her new environment. In the rough-and-tumble of adolescent debate in RE sessions and PSE periods, she would sit silently for almost a whole period, and then in a low voice, to no one particular, say, 'You are so *infantile.*' The words are so full of contempt, but the body language is crushed and weary. Her PSE tutor, who was also her RE teacher, had done some basic counselling courses, and decided to try to reflect the complex cry for help she was hearing. She needed to communicate, 'I am listening to you carefully, not judging, but accepting, saying "you are safe" and asking, "where do you want to go with this?" '

She is about to face French, too. Again, a challenge to my leadership skills: follow me, I know this subject, am well trained, know the syllabus; together we will succeed in our tasks. Is Betty sitting there, mind focused on a different task? Will we battle for control? I recall the other requirement of the leader: Betty, in pursuing this task, you will not be hurt, not be humiliated, you will be enhanced as a person. This is a safe place for you to be. Fortunately, she has received both messages from her RE/PSE teacher.

To communicate that message is a complex task. 'Betty, have you got a moment?' Not a summons, an invitation. 'I don't want to bug you or invade your privacy, but I keep getting a sense that part of you sometimes wants to shriek out, "You haven't got a clue, shut up and listen to what I want to say." And at the same time, what you want to say is so big that you daren't put it into words. I just want to say that if you *do* want to put it into words, on your own with me or in the class, that's fine. At your own pace.' This teacher is picking up and reflecting feeling. It would have been possible to go for the logic, with its adversarial tendency and to ask, 'What exactly was infantile in what they were saying?' The pupil, skilled as we all are in the use of logic to keep others at a distance, could have felt defensive, under attack and unsafe. Access to deeper, more troubling material would have become that much more difficult. Betty left the teacher's office without further disclosure, but having received the message that when she was ready, there was a non-judgemental recipient of her message awaiting her. We will meet Betty again in some case material in the next chapter – at the moment, she knows that her distress signal has been picked up.

We could go on, pupil by pupil, each one bringing social and emotional challenges of varying severity into the classroom. They are not separate or separable from the academic challenge – indeed, they impinge on it, just as the socio-emotional elements of the workplace affect absenteeism, productivity, levels of injury and safety in business. We can no more ignore the effects of the socio-emotional dimension on the achievement of task objectives than can our managerial colleagues in the commercial world. Nor, I would want to argue, would the vast majority of teachers want so to concentrate on academic objectives as to turn their back on children in pain. I happen to be writing this on 25 March 1995, a thousand miles away from my home, and as I flick through the daily *El País*, a very respectable newspaper, I note the following article about a young boy, undergoing a horrific home life, yet performing well at an academic level: 'An 8-year-old boy has been repeatedly raped by his mother, her boyfriend, his aunt's boyfriend, his great-grandparents, who are in their seventies, and other members of the family.' When teachers noted and reported his confused behaviour and inappropriate sexualizing of relationships, 'fue difícil que hablará', it was very difficult for him to talk about the experience. However, in his academic work, he was described as 'intelligent and wide awake', performing well. This is clearly an extraordinary case, but it does illustrate that children can 'go normally to school', function effectively at the academic level yet carry with them the most crushing experiences we can imagine. One hopes that the 'Leonardinos' of this world are a rarity – perhaps this lad can sensitize us to the need to 'listen beyond the words'.

Immediacy and the culture of vigilance that immediacy permits do not come easily. They require a profound self-awareness, a deep sensitivity to those with whom we are relating and the skill to communicate all that awareness in such a way that an accepting, unconditional positive regard always accompanies the precisely formulated reflection. I need to be able to say, 'In this relationship, I know who I am and I am willing to be, transparently, with you. I am intent on your communications to me, too, and will check out that the messages you are sending are received accurately by me. And I have no intention of pushing, hurrying, pressuring, investigating the "you" that you are in the relationship – my wish is to accept you.'

It is probably appropriate for me to go back to my class – a 'normal' comprehensive school group. As a French teacher, I am quite disconcerted by the foregoing. I almost feel as if I am sinking into a morass of new teaching skills that leave me feeling deskilled and apprehensive. I was so looking forward to the lesson – now I've got all this 'culture of vigilance' and immediacy buzzing around in my head. I need to touch *terra firma* again.

Terra firma, for me, is good practice. Of course we can disagree about what constitutes 'good practice' (see the vision of Lawlor cited in Chapter 2), but it does seem useful to try to incorporate the ideas of listening to cries for help into some framework familiar to us as teachers. In theoretical terms we are developmentalists. We have a vision that includes some understanding that humans 'develop' in some systematic, coherent, relatively predictable way. We may even recall distant lectures on Piaget and intellectual development, and the younger reader may have perused Donaldson's (1982) critique of Piagetian ideas. A more comprehensive approach to the idea of systematic growth and refinement of competence is offered by Blocher (1974), who suggests that 'development is seen to combine growth, maturation and learning. It is influenced by environmental factors, within whose context developmental processes must be understood. *All developmental processes are considered interrelated*' (p.63). Most of us recognize the key elements: growth, maturation, learning and the environment. We know, at least implicitly, that the young people in my French class are at certain reasonably close points in a physiological process (young, adolescents), and that a series of environmental stimuli (of which I the teacher am one) act upon the growing organism in a way that is mediated by various psychological processes; this mediation facilitates learning and maturation. The significant phrase of Blocher is that all the developmental processes are interrelated. As teachers we already operate with this model; in that sense, it in no way deskills us, but it does merit closer scrutiny.

We detect 'cries for help' in their loudest form when they are communicated by some developmental factor which fits ill with our view of the 'normal'. Our training, our experience and perhaps our values mean that our acuity as detectors of malfunctioning is probably most effective in the intellectual sphere, though the existence and continuing growth of systems of pastoral care indicates clearly that we accept (again perhaps implicitly) the interrelatedness of development. Thus, though in my French class I am intent on offering an environmental stimulus (my well-prepared lesson) to enhance the growth and maturation of the language competence of the class, knowing the interrelatedness of development I am aware that Tom, Betty and others cannot be sliced up into, for example, academic Tom, social Tom, moral Tom, emotional Tom, sexual Tom and so on.

There is Tom the person, and any attempt, conscious or otherwise, to fragment him is doomed to failure.

Two further useful concepts from the developmentalists are the 'halo' effect and the phenomenon of 'asychronicity'. Given that we develop interrelatedly across many areas, and that there is a statistically established range of competence in these areas, which allows us tentatively to talk of 'underfunctioning' and 'abnormal behaviour, we can accept that Betty may be operating in a developmentally appropriate way *intellectually*, while we may see her as underfunctioning socially and emotionally. This asynchronous development can produce the halo effect which occurs when the observer's values lead him or her to listen more carefully to behaviours that he or she deems important and to allow a halo effect to blur the sensitivity to other less significant (to her or him) factors. Put simply, Betty's (or any pupil's) competence in school work *can* blind us to other developmental areas which are interrelated and influential. To respond to that, my task in the modern languages room is extended, to include with my skills as a French teacher skills which allow me to embrace the interrelatedness of the development of my pupils. Oh, and by the way, the capital of Burundi is Bujumbura.

Exercises

The exercises related to this chapter have two major foci: the enhancing of awareness, and the ability to communicate that awareness to pupils appropriately, using the skill of immediacy. The chapter has argued that the developmental complexity of human beings can lead us to a narrow focusing on certain areas of development (e.g. academic) in a way that fails to take account of the significance of the interactive nature of all areas of development – thus academic remedial work for a pupil who is failing because of some unattended socioemotional challenge is bound to fail because it does not address the source of the difficulty. The exercises are based on the position of Perls: that by increasing our self-awareness, we gain close access to realities of our client.

I am somebody

Frequently we will say of someone, she or he seems really nice, but I don't really know her or him. We are recognizing that in human interactions we are frequently not fully in contact with the other person. It is not necessarily the case that the other person is hiding; it can be that we are not attuned to certain messages that are being sent. A good place to begin to learn to sensitize ourselves to less overt messages is in ourselves. This exercise, led by the trainer, who ought to speak in a quiet, slow tone, with pauses between each of the instructions, involves a relaxation procedure, followed by a journey inwards. (There are many good relaxation tapes, based on different physiological or psychological principles, on the market – but you can simply choose some tranquil, even pastoral, music and work as follows.)

> Can you lie comfortably, deliberately trying to relax your body completely?
> It may help to close your eyes.

Now, aware that your body is physically relaxed, allow yourself to become fully aware of your breathing. Enjoy it; breathe in as relaxed a way as possible, treating yourself to an oxygen-rich, deep inhalation if that seems comfortable. Be aware of your breathing. (Thirty seconds of silence/music.)

Little by little, allow your focus to slip away from your breathing, to fasten on some sound outside of you. Some specific element of the music, a violin, a flute, or a sound outside of the room. Fasten on to this sound – stay with it. (Thirty seconds.)

Now, very gently come back to yourself. Check your body. Is it still relaxed? Which parts are not, is somewhere cramped? Make sure you are comfortable again. Be aware of your scalp, relax it; your cheeks and jaws, and let them ease; check your neck and shoulders and if they feel tense, think them loose; your chest needs attention too – a deep breath, a stretch and a conscious relaxation; are your hands clenched? – release them; how about your tummy, pelvis and bottom; quite deliberately, and in an unhurried way, let them flop. Your legs and feet may feel tight – send thoughts down to set them free. Every part of your body is yours, to tense or relax. You may not have met parts of your body for a long time. Get to know them. They are all part of the 'you' you take into the classroom. Now increase your awareness of the physical you: pains, aches, wonderful eddies of some pleasing sensation. Your body sends messages – are you listening?

Gradually, ensuring that you feel as relaxed and refreshed as you can, allow yourself to emerge once more in this room – refreshed, aware, in touch with your body.

The group can then be invited to discuss the experience. What about their bodies? Do they feel that the opportunity to be more aware has helped or hindered their sense of self? What messages have they ignored in the past: aching shoulders, acid stomach, sore eyes, a leaping heart at the sight of someone, a warm glow in some special person's presence? Hello, body; nice to meet you.

The real me

Our body is the primary context in which we are. Beyond, within and around our physical selves, there is a complex psychological 'me' – I take my body into a room, and show those parts of the deeper me that seem appropriate. Frequently, the initial disclosure is logical, rational, controlled, defended. Only later do we feel able and ready to share our deeper selves, the sensations and visceral experiences, the values, emotions, attitudes and beliefs that are so influential on our behaviour. As with all our experiences, the level of awareness we have can vary. It is quite possible for us to carry round an influential attitude (sexism, racism) of which we are unaware, or a feeling (of inadequacy) that leaves us reluctant to raise our hand to ask a question in a public meeting, or a belief (that fate is more powerful than personal effort) which has us reluctant to try when the going gets tough. The next chapter will present a model to look at this in more detail. Here is some practical work to raise awareness. In the section on sensory awareness it is important to recognize overtly in the group that some members may have a sensory impairment. Their contributions can be invaluable in shifting our perspectives.

Sit in as relaxed a way as you can. Quite deliberately let all the thoughts, problems, decisions you currently face whiz around in your head. Do not try to select, just let them be – all of them, in all their complexity. Be aware of them, but try not to address them or work with them. Think, this is the stuff of my life. Money, relationships, work, children, more work, house repairs, car . . . What complex creatures we are. And that, too, goes into the classroom or the counselling session with us. (Three minutes.) Discuss with a partner any insights you have gained. How do you feel after the exercise? Are you sitting on things that are troubling you? Were there things that you had lost sight of, but which were still bubbling around? Is any of that material likely to get in the way of your teaching, counselling?

Now, relaxed again, let your sensations flow into awareness. Initially, it may be helpful to close your eyes. Your sense of touch. What are you now aware of from a tactile point of view? Where do your clothes touch you; comfortably, uncomfortably? Do you note sensations of heat or cold; draughts; your own breath on your upper lip; the feel of your tongue in your mouth, feet in your shoes? Explore your sense of touch. (Two minutes.)

What odours are you aware of? Pleasant, unpleasant? Are they powerful or light; do they induce recollections of things past? Search the ambience for the faintest smells: carpet, polish, hair lacquer, ink. Explore your sense of smell. (Two minutes.)

Do you have a taste in your mouth? Were you aware of it before it was mentioned? Is it pleasant or not? Old food, toothpaste, cigarette, a kiss? These tastes are also part of the real you. Explore your sense of taste. (Two minutes.)

What do you hear? Beyond my voice. Colleagues breathing? Tummies rumbling? A motor mower, birdsong outside, the chatter of others, not working? Traffic noise, music? Do you blank sound out, reduce your awareness; unconsciously, deliberately? Explore your sense of hearing. (Two minutes.)

If your eyes are closed, gently open them and become aware of what you see. Let your gaze wander; colours, shapes, tones, lightness and darkness, dimensionality, depth; focus in detail on some small item. Know it visually; master its every element. Explore your sense of sight. (Two minutes.)

Discuss in the full group the idea of awareness. Do you feel more aware? What is it like? Try to identify how it feels.

Now deeper still. Try to relax again, perhaps shutting your eyes. Allow your awareness of feelings to grow. What, now, is the feeling that is most to the fore? Just for yourself, give it a name, attach words to it. Is it located somewhere? Does it move? Is it hard to pin down? Does it have a shape, a colour, some other characteristic? Get as close to the feeling as you can. (Two minutes.)

With a partner, discuss the feeling you became aware of. Your partner's task is to listen and reflect.

By this time, most people have achieved levels of awareness which are way beyond the superficial, everyday awareness we have most of the time. It can feel uncomfortable, even overwhelming, since much of our denied or repressed material is treated that way because it is perceived as potentially damaging to us, and we can still experience that uncomfortable feeling of risk. Equally, giving this awareness words, putting it on to a conscious agenda, can feel liberating and relaxing since we no longer deploy the psychological energy needed to keep it from consciousness. Being our 'selves' fully, i.e. being congruent, frees us from the tension associated with denial. There is also a self-affirming dimension in the acceptance we give to ourselves – we give ourselves space, and value ourselves sufficiently to 'be' fully. The next exercise takes us on to our awareness of others. If we are capable of ignoring large tracts of our own being, how much more can we fail to see, turn our backs on, challenging parts of the persons we work with. Argyle (1988) tells us that as much as 60 per cent of reciprocal communication is non-verbal i.e. we tell each other things without words, and much important communication occurs 'beyond the words'. He also tells us that such is the power of the non-verbal input that if there is a discrepancy between the words said and the bodily communication, we pay more attention to the non-verbal input. This includes cries for help, and suggests that we need to develop awareness here, too. I first experienced the following exercise when the group was being led by a colleague, Peter Cook, and am grateful to him for sharing it with me and, through me, the reader.

The hidden you

This exercise will be done in threes. Each sub-group will consist of a communicator, a receiver and an observer. If there is time, each person can take a turn in each role, but that is not essential. The task of the communicators is to draw to mind some intense experience from the past – distant or recent, pleasant or unpleasant – which they are willing to explore. The example I give is of learning, as a child, to dive. I still recall the apprehension of throwing myself head first into the void, the preparation, the act, the delight in 'flying', the relief, the pride and so on. When the 'incident' is chosen, the communicator and receiver sit facing each other, and take hold of each other's right hand in a light 'handshake' position, but with the arms of both at rest, on their knee. No prior information on the incident is given. The observer takes up a position which allows clear sight of the communicator – unobtrusive note-taking may be helpful. When all are comfortably in position, the communicator, with eyes closed and in silence, mentally relives the chosen experience, indicating that the process has begun by gently squeezing the hand of the receiver. In two or three minutes, when the experience is ended, all can relax. While it is occurring, the receiver and the observer (who may want to write) must become intensely aware of the non-verbal communication of the communicator, which, as is evident in the exercise, is apparently minimal.

After a short rest, the same communicator is asked to choose a different incident, and to relive it, following the same procedures as in the first one. Again the receiver and observer watch carefully. Again a short rest, then a third, final incident is requested, following the same procedure. Thus within about ten minutes, one person has relived three different intense experiences, while being closely observed by two colleagues.

The final task for the communicator is to choose one of the three, without telling the two colleagues which, and to repeat it, observed in the same way as before. The observer and receiver are then asked to identify which of the three was repeated. The only information they have is the non-verbal communication of the subject. It is my experience that participants are highly skilled in making a correct identification – and further, that having been asked to explore further, they can identify that 'it was a happy/sad/catastrophic etc. incident'. On one occasion, the receiver and observer had noticed that it was a painful experience, and that 'You kept swallowing and rubbing your left leg. Was it some kind of accident?' The communicator had been reliving a motor cycle accident.

Perhaps most important is the full group discussion following the exercise. It is very evident that the observation skills are there, and that what is necessary is a pressure to bring them to awareness. Participants notice eyelid flickering, swallowing, neck pulse changes, grip changes, palm temperature, chewing, smiles, leg and body movements, respiration and so on. Clearly, to go through life subjecting our companions to that kind of attention could well lead to considerable tension; the exercise is an indicator of how much non-verbal material we receive, our skill at picking it up and using it, and the variable level of awareness which attends it.

So far we have looked at strategies for increasing our self awareness, our sensitivity to those around us, and we now move on to an exercise which looks at what we do with that awareness – it is an exercise in immediacy.

This exercise is done with a partner. Find a relatively private space, and begin by individually writing down three similarities between you and your partner and three differences. Try to avoid the obvious (we both wear glasses, you are a man and I am a woman), and use your awareness of and sensitivity to the other. It doesn't matter if you get it wrong. When both have produced a list, share the similarities, and talk about where the perceptions have come from. Are you noticing the non-verbal messages that come from clothing ('We're both informal, not too bothered about appearances'), jewellery ('You like beautiful artefacts, I think I am more taken with countryside and nature'), the body ('We both look people in the eye'), tones of voice ('I think we can both be assertive, even aggressive'). Discuss what it feels like to do this exercise. Easy to identify the elements, but hard to communicate them? Anxiety about being wildly wrong? Occasionally, participants will say that they do not know each other well enough to participate, yet it is the case that a head can land in the staffroom at break and announce, 'Can I briefly introduce *everyone to Mr Don Helm. You'll all get to know him as the year goes on – he's the new LEA inspector for information technology across the curriculum.' Don smiles and, following the head, retreats to the china and expensive chocolate biscuits of the head's office. The momentary silence following the withdrawal is punctuated by someone's 'Ho! I didn't like the look of him!' Yes, we do have immediate responses – and this exercise is to get inside of them and look at how they work.*

To conclude: awareness and sensitivity are powerful tools. Used insensitively they can lead the recipient to feel harassed, corralled, overwhelmed. Egan talks about our winning the right to challenge, after having created a climate of trust. We must not bang people over the head with our 'sensitivity'! Bear in mind, too, that the use of the 'beyond the words' reflections that can come from enhanced awareness needs to be tentative: 'I get the impression . . .', 'I may be off target here, but you seem to . . .', 'Those tears seem to indicate that there is still a lot of hurt, although you say you are OK.' At all times, the wisdom of the client leads the direction and the pace. Sometimes, it will not feel safe enough to let go of the denial.

CHAPTER 6

Understanding the challenge: working with deep feelings

Everything that has been explored so far can justifiably be applied to the classroom teacher: the central need to free the pupil from anxiety about the integrity of 'self', so that there is plenty of psychological energy to explore, to seek stimulation, to risk, to learn; the obligation to create a climate of safety within which to listen both to the words of the pupils and to those messages which seep out sometimes barely consciously beyond any words. The intention of all this is not, as we have seen, to turn the teacher into some all-seeing, all-perceiving big brother (or *pace* Orwell, sister), it is rather to communicate to the young person that she or he is of such value that she or he merits that kind of attention. The attention is supportive, not evaluative; it is meticulously non-invasive, but always gently communicated as being available. The available research evidence clearly indicates that all this happens to the extent to which the teaching relationship is infused by the core conditions – and, ominously, that to the extent that such a relationship is not available, pupils and clients will retreat into the pseudo-safety of the denials and defences that have proved useful fortifications in past encounters with the unrespectful, the intrusive, the judgemental adult.

Good teachers have always deployed the basic skills of the counsellor. They may not have used the same language to describe their activity, but they saw teaching as essentially a liberating activity, freeing the talents of the pupils to bloom in an atmosphere of support. And yes, that does sound almost corny, and I have spent enough time with the 'f*** off' brigade to know that some pupils are, for whatever reason, so deeply damaged that any progress occurs in millimetres, and seems to involve as much sliding back as going forward. At the same time, I have had the privilege of watching teachers perform daily miracles with such pupils, precisely by operating beyond their academic skills with the skills of the counsellor.

So what, if any, are the differences between the work of the highly skilled teacher and that of the counsellor? I would like to present a model of personality based on several different editions of *Therapeutic Psychology* (Brammer and Shostrum, 1968, 1977, 1982; Brammer *et al.*, 1989) to try to get at the point at which the two skills separate. I suggest it is not in the quality of the relationship we all seek, nor fundamentally in the skills deployed, but in the depth at which we work. It is a question of the process of counselling. Depth, of course, is a metaphor used to suggest that the material being worked on by the client is less accessible, more protected, perhaps even denied altogether. It is personal material that has an impact on the way the client is living, but which has been tucked away as too frightening, too potentially explosive to allow to the surface. And if it can blow up a client, what on earth might it do to me, the counsellor? Deep material belonging to the client, on, for example, loss, sexuality, self-worth, authority and autonomy, will *always* touch my own material in those areas. What unresolved issues of loss are around for me, how comfortable am I with my own sexuality, do I feel secure, really, in my sense of self, what attitudes towards authority and personal autonomy drive my behaviour? To work at depth with clients on such material, I am, in Egan's (1986) challenging phrase, professionally obliged to 'come to terms with the problematic in the self' – my self. Not all teachers want to do that, or have the space to do so. This is the point at which the counsellors and the teachers diverge.

Let me give an example of what I mean by depth. Imagine a careers interview with a 16-year-old wondering what to do next (Figure 6.1). Basically she or he is trying to decide whether to stay on to Year 11 and possibly 12, or to leave and go on a training scheme. She or he may start talking at a rational, logical level which the teacher will listen to, reflect, summarize and clarify, helping her or him to weigh up 'money now' against future possibilities; an immediate contribution to the family budget and a future potential one. The teacher will not impose, judge, direct, but try to facilitate the pupil's decision-making (more of that in Chapters 7 and 8). Given the support of a 'counselling' relationship in the encounter, the pupil may feel able to divulge material at a different level, perhaps sharing values, and the teacher's job develops beyond exploring the logical feasibilities to helping the pupil to do some value clarification. This is not to arrive at some established 'orthodoxy'; it is a real exploration of the values of the pupil. As the session goes on (or perhaps at a different session) and the sense of safety grows, the pupil can quite suddenly swoop into quite startling, deep material: 'The fact is I am absolutely terrified of my dad' or 'I've never said this to anyone, miss. But my dad messes with me, and I'll do anything to get out of the house.'

Deep material from clients can elicit from listeners their own call for help: what unexamined parts of me are touched by this client's disclosure? A look of shock, disgust, horror can hit the client with great force, leaving him or her deeply regretting the decision to disclose – we do need to come to terms with the problematic in our selves. I recall doing a training day in which I argued that, if counsellors needed to be able to stand close to the deep feelings of their clients, they needed first to have stood close to their own deep feelings. Someone in the audience later came to see me for counselling, because 'everyone I've seen so far is even more scared of me than I am'. Deep material is powerful and therefore scary, which is why counsellor training spends so long on the personal development of trainees' comfort with, access to and familiarity with their own material.

Brammer and Shostrum suggest that our personality can be imagined as having the layered characteristics of an onion. Figure 6.1 offers an initial, simple view of what that might mean in practical terms. But let us take it a little further. Each of us, they suggest, displays to the world an 'outer defence system'. It is a permeable defence: unless we are paranoid, we let others pass through it, when it feels safe, to gain access to the top layers of the self that lie behind it. In the classroom, 31 outer defence systems, mine and my 30 French pupils', are at the ready. The timetable says French, but the real game is called 'risk'. We are all reasonably healthy individuals, and we are aware of a mutual capacity for hurt. We test the water, risking, in small measure, to see what happens. If all is well then we open the permeable outer defence system further. If someone (it doesn't have to be me) gets hurt, everyone becomes that bit less permeable. Figure 6.2 indicates that, to the extent that we feel safe, we permit access to the next layer, the ego system, which is that part of the person that is concerned with environmental mastery, being in control, safe; it is rational, logical. For us as teachers that usually feels OK, but imagine the risk to pupil self-esteem if they allow a bright, university-educated adult in there. Before they do, they will make pretty sure you are not going to create havoc and humiliation. As a young teacher I was always terrified that someone would ask me a word I did not know. I protected myself by engaging in what I now know was 'ego-defensive teaching' – a well-nigh impermeable outer defence system that did not let them through with questions. My teacher role did not allow me not to know, so I carefully controlled lessons so that they usually stayed within my knowledge base. I recall, still with embarrassment, being caught short on French vocabulary when a pupil, writing about his job aspirations, asked, 'Sir, my dad's a builder. What's "pulley" in French?' Oh, sugar; they got me!

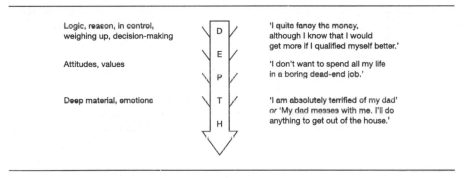

Figure 6.1 Disclosure and depth

To empathize with the pupils and their outer defence system, it is probably useful to think of cross-school INSET days. We are suddenly in a teacher's centre, about to spend a practical morning on . . . We eye up the opposition, er, make that colleagues. A pretty bright-looking bunch. Best if I just keep my head down, look wise and say nowt. Where did I learn that? Well, blow me, it was years ago in Year 9, or the fifth form as it then was. A good teacher, or INSET leader, will be aware, as has been constantly emphasized, that tasks will not be fully addressed when the key issue of organismic safety is unresolved. Creating a learning environment is the first task of the good teacher, and it rarely happens by accident.

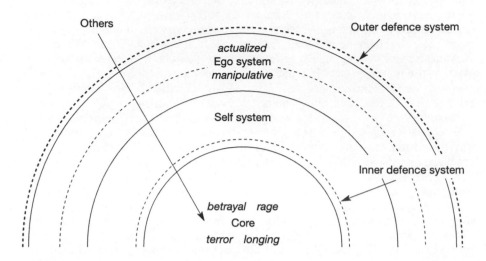

Figure 6.2 A depth model of personality

Let us imagine that it has been achieved, and that the interpenetration of the persons in the group begins. Think of the first exchanges: guarded, rational, controlled, courteous. Few people will say, 'How do you do, I'm gay', or 'a Catholic', or 'in the throes of a divorce'. We tend to the ego system communication of, 'How do you do, I'm Jones from Wadham High; biology.' Note the difference between that and 'How do you do, I'm the head of biology at Wadham High.' The second *could* be a manipulative (see Figure 6.2) statement about personal status, and deeper, related material. Thus, the logic and rationality of our ego system can be deployed in an 'actualized' way, i.e. genuinely, transparently, without a covert agenda, or 'manipulatively', when the communication is devious, sending out layered, double messages that confuse the recipient and create a climate of mistrust. We are frequently not aware (awareness again) of the manipulative nature of our ego-level relating. Berne (1961, 1972) offers a different theoretical explanation in transactional analysis, but we can see the double message in this apparently logical exchange:

> *Husband:* I can't find a clean shirt. Where have you put them?
> *Wife:* Where I always put them, in the airing cupboard.

The apparently straightforward communication of shirt location is layered next to a further communication of, 'Stupid, how do you have to ask that after all these years?' Our capacity for double messages is high, and immensely powerful.

Slightly deeper disclosures do occur with relative ease. Our INSET leader might try to create opportunity for such more intimate disclosure, for example, by using the ice-breaking exercises of Chapter 1. 'What fears or anxieties are you feeling in this group at the moment?' It *is* a different kind of communication; we feel it, we know it, and some of us may decide to opt out. It is too intrusive, inappropriate, not time, too soon. This greater depth takes us into the self system, sometimes referred to as 'the real me'. It is the part of our personality wherein reside our values, attitudes, beliefs, feelings and emotions; and we like to keep it pretty private, as do our pupils. To share at this level requires courage, generosity, a feeling that the disclosure will not be misused – the 'real me' is worth protecting. The process of counselling involves a journey, at a speed determined by the client, inwards, gradually raising to the level of the conscious all the material that has been running our behaviour, half in our awareness, for such a time. The most able teachers will recall occasions when pupils have shared 'the real me' – it is a very positive comment from the pupil about the quality of the relationship established by that teacher, when feelings, values and attitudes are shared. And there is further to go.

When, at INSET days, teachers express reservations about counselling, discussion usually reveals a fear that they will loose some dreadful monster. Chapter 1 acknowledges that in practice teachers, however committed and skilled, will not be able to offer specialist counselling unless they are timetabled to do it. Nevertheless, it is useful for us all to have some theoretical peg on which to hang disturbing and disturbed behaviour in our children. It is reassuring that teachers have an awareness of the potential for harm, and the model of Brammer and Shostrum can offer us insight into where that potential comes from. At the deepest levels of our personality, they suggest, is an area of powerful feelings that each of us perceives as having great destructive power – to which area we consign material that has deeply affected us in the past. For each of us it is unique. We contain that material within the 'inner defence system', this time a system to protect us from attack from the inside, not the outside. Why do some of us have desperate palpitations, dry mouth and sweaty palms as we rise to challenge the head at a staff meeting? What makes some of us terrified of water, flying, men, women? Where does the feeling of dread as we see leaves falling in the autumn come from? Well, the behaviourists would say that we have learned that such a response is rewarding; the Freudians would tell us that it results from the frustration of early libidinal impulses, which gets transformed into neurotic symptoms, which can be reactivated as we go through life. All very interesting, but for us as counsellors, the interpretive, explanatory dimension is not our central concern; our aim is to help the client to gain access to the material in her or his person which is hurting, reducing effectiveness, depressing, diminishing. Sometimes that material is inside the inner defence system. Those of us whose work is primarily teaching can certainly work at the levels nearer the surface with pupils, and, understanding the personality model, may well feel less threatened as we refer pupils to those with more counselling time and expertise.

It must be said that many people carry such material around indefinitely; they do not seek or want help, and some idea that we must ferret around inside people's psyche to 'liberate' such material is totally misconceived. When, and if, a client begins to explore some difficulty, and if the process of counselling, the journey undertaken by the client, takes us into that material, then the counsellor will, as in all phases of counselling, be at the client's side, reflecting, checking: 'Is this where you are, is this what you are saying, is this the direction in which you are headed?' This essential posture of the counsellor makes it impossible for accusations of implantation of material (see recent debates on the 'false memory syndrome' and sexual abuse: British Psychological Society, 1995) to be sustained. One further point: the idea that we will accidentally set free some monster fails to take into account the powerful psychological mechanisms the client has in place to contain that material. It also fails to take into account the essential role of the counsellor as reflective of the wishes of the client; we should not be initiators. Core material is held secure because the client sees it as potentially destructive, and will approach it only when she or he feels that it is safe to do so. This feeling will occur only after long, client-centred exploration with a highly skilled counsellor. Rogers's phrase the 'wisdom of the client' again comes to mind; access to deep material will occur when the client deems it safe. In a moving counselling session with a leukaemia sufferer, Rogers so facilitates the client's search that he approaches what he describes as 'a pit of green slime' – his core. He does not access the material, describes himself as 'walking around it', not wanting even to dip a foot in. Rogers, after the film, talks of the 'wisdom of his client' in determining the pace of the process (Concorde Films, 201 Felixstowe Road, Ipswich, Suffolk IP3 9BJ).

We have now certainly moved beyond the basic counselling skills of the classroom teacher, but we are not on some distant planet that bears no comparison to our own. All those highly skilled initial contacts, those facilitative relationships created, the ambience of safety and respect, are required of both the classroom teacher and the counsellor. In addition, we carry our own core material into the classroom, and it may be that it flows inappropriately into our work. The foregoing can at least raise our awareness of that possibility. It can also alert us to the possibility that some of the children who respond to our basic counselling ability will need to be referred for various reasons to the specialist counsellor. I propose to offer a critical analysis of case material to illustrate the journey we have made. It is not an actual case – for ethical reasons that is not possible – but it is a composite of real elements drawn from the literature and my own practice. I have chosen a case of sexual abuse for two reasons: first, it is a sadly common trauma faced by many of our children; second, it is a trauma that is very difficult to work with.

> *Mary's first contact with her year head was the result of a referral following an expression of concern by her language teacher that her work had suddenly begun to deteriorate. She was approaching 17, and was in the opening phase of her university preparation, having done very well in her GCSEs. The initial conversations, sensitively conducted by Mary's head of year, led Mary to disclose that she was not sleeping well and had lots of headaches. She also felt constantly nauseous and ate little. This was not yet a counselling relationship, though the head of year was using counselling skills.*

The head of year, having listened and reflected carefully, properly saw the first requirement as a medical check, and suggested to Mary that she might want to see her GP. Mary seemed quite happy to do this, and returned to say the doctor had said it was stress, and that she ought to take more exercise, relax more and keep her work in perspective. She looked tired and drawn, and her language teacher said she had lost her sparkle.

> *The second contact was the result of Mary being found crying in the toilets, inconsolable, by another pupil, who had sought the help of a teacher. 'I just feel awful; I hate myself; I want to die,' she eventually said to the year head, a*

warm, supportive woman in her forties. The year head was worried and suggested that Mary might like to talk to David Potter, the recently appointed school counsellor. She was not at all keen to do this, and the year head emphasized that there was no obligation whatsoever. Her tears had stopped and she was talking quite lucidly, and suddenly said, 'I think I ought to go and see Mr Potter.' Thus began the contact with the specialist.

David Potter had worked as a science teacher before deciding to do an MA in counselling. His recent appointment to the school had raised eyebrows, and he felt this as a pressure to 'perform'. He had already worked with a number of pupils to people's satisfaction, but he suspected that this case would be long and demanding. He had been particularly struck by the year head's report that the girl had said, 'I hate myself.' David was consoled that his task was not to ferret out a truth, but to stay with his client, as she made decisions about the journey she wished to make.

The first two sessions were characterized by relationship building. David assiduously listened, reflected accurately, summarized at intervals and picked out a number of emerging themes. He was non-evaluating, and worked hard to communicate his full acceptance of the client. Mary told him of her loss of interest in work, 'in everything'. His reflection that 'You have no interest in anything?' brought a wry smile to the lips of this intelligent young woman: 'Well, I wouldn't be here if I wasn't interested in anything at all, would I?' David, listening carefully, was able to reflect non-judgementally, 'So you are interested in something, and that brings you here, is that right?' A nod. 'Can you tell me what the something is?' A silence, then 'I'm not sure, I think it's me.' David smiled, 'You're here because of you.' Assent from the client, and a further long silence. David does not hurry things, waits, and then: 'I have a sense that the "me" that brings you here is very confused, and that you don't know where to start. And I just want to say there is no rush.' That space and removal of pressure seemed important. The client seemed to see her counsellor as a haven of safety, in which she could really look at any aspects of that complex 'me' she brought to the sessions. 'Have a look at this,' she said, and pushed up her left sleeve. There were about eight scars, like a ladder, going up towards the inner elbow. 'I did that,' she said gravely. (All the thoughts of, 'How silly', 'Why did you do that?', 'You could have really damaged yourself', flooded into David's mind – his agenda, his evaluation, the phrases that would lock her shut again, proof against interrogation, and punishment.) 'You did it to yourself?', he said, hoping that it came out as a statement, not a judgement. Again the nod. She was testing – this man is not going to pass judgement on me. 'I just wanted to tell my body how much I hate it. It's not like my body, anyway.' David, aware with great immediacy of a host of thoughts about self-harm and sex abuse, calmly stayed with Mary's agenda. 'In some sense, the body you're in doesn't feel like yours.'

The detail of the session is now less significant than the fact that, slowly (so slowly for a counsellor knowing his colleagues want results, and quickly), Mary was able to go to some deep material and share it with her counsellor. This could have happened with the head of year; it depends on the client's perception of the extent to which she is truly accepted. She was, indeed, being sexually abused, and had been since the age of 9. Having told David, she also recounted her several attempts to tell other teachers during her time as a victim: 'They didn't seem as if they would understand.' As David suspected, it was the beginning of a long and arduous counselling process.

Using the model of Brammer and Shostrum presented above, and prescinding from the specific case of Mary, it is possible to look at how the journey typically is made – though of course, each person has a unique pain to bear. Figure 6.3 indicates the path.

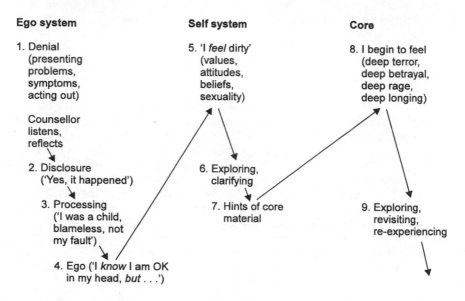

Figure 6.3 The victim of sexual abuse: typical stages

To represent the agony of sexual abuse in a diagram is inevitably and woefully inadequate, and I must hasten to add that the complexity of a single, unique case would show that inadequacy. The usefulness of the diagram is to give a kind of overview of process; not all victims will pass through each stage, nor will each stage be as clinically distinct from the previous one as on the printed page, but relating the stages to the model offered by Brammer and Shostrum, we are able to get our heads around one of the most difficult counsellor challenges to be faced.

1. Denial. It is frequently the case that the presenting problem for the victim of abuse will not be a disclosure of abuse. Changes in the quality of school work, behaviour with peers or teachers, eating disorders, self-mutilation can all be the first cry for help. It is crucial, however, that neither teachers nor counsellors should become 'diagnostic', drawing conclusions or making interpretations about possible trauma based on presenting problems. Both as teachers and as counsellors our task here is to listen, reflect, go at the pace and in the direction of the client. This is easy to say, and very hard to do. It requires a careful use of the basic skills of counselling.

2. Disclosure. When clients have been allowed in a non-judgemental climate to explore the meaning of the 'symptoms' (usually some behaviour which is self-diminishing), from their own phenomenological perspective, they may decide it is time to dive deeper, and pull from the depths some element of their pain; perhaps a statement that they are being abused. They will make this decision when it feels safe enough to do so, and the creation of that safety is a key task of the adult with whom they are talking – at this stage it may be either a teacher or a counsellor. Deep material will touch our own deep material, so preparatory work by teachers and counsellors would have them exploring the problematic in themselves: what issues of sexuality are raw for me; can I block this or other issues by gaze aversion, looks of shock or disgust, inappropriate reassurance?

3. Processing. Continually working on the agenda presented by the client, the counsellor (for normally by this time the client will be working with a counsellor) will help the client to explore the events that have been disclosed. The client will, little by little, 'tell the story', articulating material which previously was too painful to turn into words. A lot of the work will be done at the ego level as the client, working on the material reflected back by the counsellor, is often able to place the events in a logical context: 'I was a victim, it wasn't my fault, I was just a child, I carry no blame for what happened.'

4. Ego. The client concludes this phase 'knowing' that the responsibility for the pain lies elsewhere: it is not a punishment, a debt paid for her fault. This is not a position imposed by the counsellor (saying, 'but of course you can't blame yourself'), it is the result of meticulous and skilled reflection of what the client brings to the encounter. 'Yes, I hear that. You are saying that he started when you were very young, only 7 or 8. And if I hear correctly, you can recall feeling totally powerless, as if you had no ability to do anything to stop it.' She may continue, 'He was so strong, but I didn't say stop.' The counsellor, trying to stay close: 'I'm not quite sure – are you saying you think you ought to have said "stop"?' 'Yes.' 'And you didn't.' 'No.' What a temptation here to burst in with our agenda, our evaluation: 'But how could you? You were a child, he is to blame.' But no, where is the client? She is not sure if she is to blame, what responsibility she has, and she needs to make that exploration herself. 'So you didn't say stop, and you think you should have. How do you feel about it at this moment?' 'I *know* that I couldn't do anything, but I still *feel* bad.' The client has journeyed through the ego system, and is hovering at a much more demanding territory, the self – with its values, attitudes, feelings and emotions.

5. Feeling. The counsellor's own feelings will almost certainly be in play now. What are my sexual values? Whether male or female, what exploitative encounters have I had, to what extent have I used and abused others, not only sexually? Am I disgusted by what has happened to this young person? Do I find myself wanting to apportion blame, make judgements, even withdraw? Do I find myself partially titillated by the detail? Am I comfortable as we go, psychologically hand in hand, into greater depths. What are my beliefs about sex? Do I tend to the hedonistic or the puritanical? Do I see myself as well centred? Have I had sexual experiences that have left me wounded, with a residue of unresolved material? Does that flow into all my thinking in this area? Have I explored that area of personal problematic professionally? The requirement to have regular supervision facilitates the kind of exploration identified in the issues raised above. Nor is this raised to suggested that the counsellor needs somehow to rise above the rest of the world in some kind of secular sainthood; it simply draws attention to the need to stand close to our own self, before we stand close to the self of others. If we do not do that, we may find ourselves using a counselling encounter to work on our own unresolved material, rather than on the material presented by the client. Countertransference exists! It seems important, too, to recognize here that the process of general value clarification, exploration of beliefs, acceptance of feeling and emotion, all occur in school beyond and prior to any counselling. Personal and social education, tutorial work, RE, poetry, art and music all help to create an ambience which, while it includes the rational, goes beyond it. For all of us, a degree of self exploration is salutary; for the counsellor, it is a professional requirement.

6. *Exploring, clarifying.* The counsellor's task is to help the client to explore the feeling that, though I logically know I am whole, blameless, a victim, I still feel that I contributed in some way to what happened. Again, the temptation to rescue is high, but again, the 'wisdom of the client' is telling us that she needs to check for herself where she stands in this. The counsellor can leap back into logic, in a way seeking security in it, but thereby denying the next stage of the journey into the feelings that lie beneath that logic: reflection, advanced-level empathy (i.e. hearing beyond the words to themes, patterns, inconsistencies) and staying as ever with the client agenda. 'So, you are saying that though your head is quite clear that you were not to blame, there is some feeling deep inside that you were?' That is the current agenda. That is exactly where the client is, and where I, as counsellor, must be too. How on earth can a child feel responsible for being raped? Well, several adult victims have described that, contrary to all logic, they emerge from their terrifying experience feeling partly responsible (Murgatroyd and Woolf, 1982). Anything from an involuntary orgasm to a manipulative five pounds left on a child's bedside table 'to get yourself something nice' creates a sensation of complicity. The confusion of loving the perpetrator and hating the experience, too, needs to be faced head on. This is exhausting territory for both the client and the counsellor. If it is ducked, then a mass of significant material can lie, churning around to emerge in more destructive symptoms at a later time. The client by this time will be disclosing material to the counsellor, desperate, finally, to have someone to help her to exorcize the deep ghosts. It is important that we do not stray from the client's agenda.

7. *Hints of core material.* The inner defence system will try to maintain the enclosure of the deepest material – after all, it is perceived as having such destructive potential as to eliminate the self entirely. If I am to survive, this material must be locked away. Nevertheless, as the counselling relationship continues, the client may begin to allow small 'escapes' of that material – she will be checking its power, and the capacity of the counsellor to stay with it. I recall one client saying to me that she thought she had buried rage of such intensity 'that it would sweep everything away; you as well.' She was testing me, wondering whether I might say, 'Well, in that case, maybe we can let sleeping dogs lie.' She would have quite welcomed my taking the decision for her. I tried to be immediate and genuine: 'Yes, that sounds pretty powerful rage – almost scary. It almost makes me want to avoid looking at it, but only almost. I want you to know that I'm willing to give it a go if you want to follow it to its origins, even though we both know that will be very tough.' She was like the client of Rogers, walking round the pit of green slime, wondering whether

to dip a toe in or keep walking. Nor is it only rage. You will note in the representation of the Brammer and Shostrum model that at the core they suggest four elemental emotions – betrayal, terror, rage and longing – and it has been a pretty constant experience for me that abuse victims will have material related to each element. The counsellor will need to accompany the client as she confronts the ultimate *betrayal*, the total developmental insult of being raped by the person who is charged with her protection, in whom she has such faith; the *terror* that accompanies the realization that the centre of security in my universe is in reality a source of pain and hurt; the *rage* at being subjected to that betrayal and terror; the intense, almost cosmic *longing* for a relationship of safety, non-exploitative love and unconditional positive regard. All of these will be fierce, experientially demanding parts of the counselling that cannot be intellectualized until they have been accessed, touched and exorcized. To stay close to the client while this courageous effort is made requires courage, too, in the counsellor, for it will touch the counsellor's own experiences of rage, terror, betrayal and longing. Thus in the exercises at the end of this chapter we will be offered the invitation to begin our own journey inward – as with the client, always at our own pace, and to the depth that we decide.

Before we move on to that work, it is important to remind teachers and counsellors that OFSTED expects all schools to have clearly laid down procedures for dealing with abuse cases. Local authorities, too, have clearly laid down lines of communication and recommendations for liaison between police, social and education services. *Schools and their staff must familiarize themselves with these protocols*. In this case study, precisely because it is the least analysed aspect of the school's response to the abused pupil, I have deliberately concentrated on the micro-elements of the dynamic between counsellor and client. Around that interaction exist all the school's pastoral skills in symptom identification, first aid, sensitive referral, and ongoing monitoring and support (for helpful detail on this aspect of the challenge see Maher, 1987, 1990)

Exercises

Working at depth with a client makes very heavy demands on our ability to create a sufficiently secure environment for them to confront material they have denied or repressed for years. The key skills for achieving that kind of safety have been looked at in Chapter 5; in these exercises, we will address a different challenge to the counsellor. Powerful, repressed and denied issues in the client can trigger in the counsellor his or her own personal unresolved material in the same area. Thus, the sexually abused young person will shine a light on my own sexual history and the attitudes I currently have; those who have been bereaved will take me back to my own losses of loved ones; a client who is being bullied can touch longstanding material which has its seeds in my experience of feeling small and in the control of others. In a real sense, the *topic/issue* approach to categorizing counselling is a red herring; the key dimension of counselling in sexual matters, bereavement, bullying, old age, AIDS, families and so on is not a knowledge base about those topics (although that may help). The real issue is how the topics touch me as a person; what deep recesses of me do they challenge? In order to stand close to the client as she or he seeks the courage to confront the 'demons', I need to have plucked up the courage to make a similar courageous step to face my own 'demons'. Egan's challenge is unequivocal: to be with clients in this stage of deep exploration, we must have tried to come to terms with 'the problematic in ourselves'. Given the demanding nature of this level of training for counsellors, the exercises should be undertaken only in situations and with people that make you feel safe – this would normally include an experienced trainer. It is important, too, to acknowledge that such exercises may seem to undervalue the unique and indescribable agony of any in the group who may have suffered deeply. It feels appropriate to acknowledge that pain and its unique character, and to apologize if the exercise seems trivial alongside it.

Journey into inner space

Individually, write on a piece of paper two lists of the initials of people from your past, identified as follows. List one: think carefully to draw to your mind the person who at this moment is most notably a negative influence on your sexuality, who in some way diminishes it, threatens it, confuses it. Then, tracking back in time from today, identify a list of any individuals who have had a similarly powerful negative influence on your development of a sense of a sexual self. This may well not involve any abuse in a criminal sense (I hope not), but it may. Only disclose material that it feels OK to disclose. Each group member will finish up with one facet of her or his sexual development. Without identifying the initials, share your list with a trusted partner, and explore how these negative influences might flow into your life – and counselling practice – now. Try to explore the deep feelings that could be touched in you.

Then repeat the exercise, to complete the picture by looking at the other facet, this time identifying the people who have had a positive influence on your developing sexuality – again starting with today. Whom, at this moment, do I see as helping me to value, clarify, enhance my sexuality? Again, share the insights gained with a trusted partner, looking at the deep material you have accessed in the exercise, and perhaps comparing the impact of the two influences you have identified.

The material engendered in this exercise takes counsellors firmly, and supportively, into their own sexuality – a crucial first step before working with clients in this area. I need to ask, am I sexually exploitative? To what extent? Am I embarrassed, ashamed, unwilling to be genuinely open to the client's material? Could I countertransfer my own unconsidered agenda on to the client? It is sometimes the case that adults find adolescent sexuality difficult to face. Is that a leftover of my own adolescence? Do I have some personal development work to do there? It is essential that a trainer be available to help anyone who is shocked, overwhelmed or otherwise stressed by material that is unearthed.

CHAPTER 7

Emerging into daylight: options and choosing

Mary's trauma, looked at in detail in Chapter 6, is a powerful reminder of the demands made of counsellors. It also takes us to the heart of the counselling process, in that it acknowledges the *depth* at which much traumatizing material lies. It is also an opportune time at which to take stock. We have seen so far that *all* teachers, in recognition of the impact that the socio-emotional has on lifestyle in general, and academic performance in particular, have an ethical obligation to enhance their awareness of and skills in this part of pupil development. An analogy has been drawn with the doctor's obligation to have acute sensitivity to the side effects of drug prescription – like doctors, teachers must scrutinize all the effects of their professional activity. Not to do so is unprofessional in the sense that it permits unexamined and accidental effects of our professional practice as teachers to occur. Then, we have seen that beyond the prophylactic impact of such reflective teaching, schools will have to respond to the special emotional and social needs of a range of damaged children, and that for this, in addition to the skills of the teacher, pupils will need the attention of the counsellor. It is clear that no teacher with a normal teaching timetable could respond to the desperate needs of Mary in the previous chapter. In addition, working at such depth with a client does make the kind of demands on the *person* of the counsellor that specialist training is necessary, beyond the training of the teacher.

So what is counselling? Is it really different from teaching? The first question is as unanswerable as the questions 'what is medicine?' and 'what is education?' They invoke such complex issues, are such non-homogeneous concepts, that the detailed descriptive analysis of the previous pages is necessary to begin even to approach the answer. However, now that we have scrutinized a great deal of exemplar material, a summary of the plot so far will provide a launch pad for the final section.

We have seen that one way into the complexities is to examine the concept from three points of view:

● as a relationship which has special qualities;
● as a process which follows a regular pattern;
● as a body of skills and techniques.

The 'special relationship' is characterized by what research has identified as a number of crucial elements, now called the 'core conditions for effective counselling': unconditional positive regard (a communication to the individual of her or his unique dignity and value); empathy (the ability to enter the phenomenological world of the pupil, accepting and working with that reality, rather than on my own agenda); genuineness (the willingness to be fully myself in the counselling encounter, in the awareness that if I present a fearful, self-protective facade to my client, that is what the client will give back to me); and immediacy (the acute sensitivity the counsellor must have to the 'here and now' reality of the encounter, with that subtle combination of observation skills and non-threatening sharing of those observations). A relationship characterized by these core conditions is, Rogers (1942) suggests, necessary for and facilitative of client growth. Clearly, it merits the most careful analysis and professional attention.

We have also followed the 'process' of the journey undertaken by the client within that special relationship. Pupils are supported, liberated and facilitated in such a way that movement from challenge to response, problem to resolution, dysfunction to function, pain to comfort can take place. So, though the quality of the relationship is seen as the crucial, defining characteristic of counselling, it is its outcome as a 'process facilitator' that attracts us as teachers. Looking at the concept of counselling, then, as a process, we have seen that it helps a progression from the initial cry for help to the supply of help and the eventual alleviation of the dysfunction. Pupils' cries for help are about feelings of incompetence, unhappiness, dissatisfaction, anxiety, fears, anger and longing, and in general terms they will follow a series of stages to cope with their difficulty via counselling. Of course, it needs to be acknowledged that human beings are enormously resilient, sometimes declining help or facing an unavoidable pain, and that sometimes all we can do is simply 'be there' for the pupil – the support given to hurting children by teachers is an educational treasure that must not be overlooked or undervalued.

We have seen that the first phase, of exploration, requires the counsellor to create the kind of climate in which the pupil will learn to trust, and, using that trust, to explore and disclose the material that is causing concern. Sometimes that material is so deep that even the client is not initially able to say what it is. The counsellor, therefore, has to restrain his or her solution-focused dash, to give the client confidence and space to define the real issue. This will occur when the client is helped to feel safe; the creation of a safe, nurturing, caring environment is the key task of the counsellor at this stage of the process. The counsellor will achieve this by communicating the core conditions mentioned above, and via the skills of closely attending (no glancing at the watch, taking phone calls, listening and marking), accurately listening (not drifting off into speculative problem-solving, moralizing, evaluating, comparing, guessing) and reflecting the client's agenda (not pushing one's own curiosity, expertise, views, solutions into the agenda). The full focus is the pupil. Not all teachers will either want, or be able, to engage at this level, but this does not preclude them from the helping process. To infuse my classroom, my conversations with pupils, my playground encounters with the core conditions – respect, empathy, genuineness and immediacy – difficult though this is, is in itself to offer the kind of ambience within which the Rogerian concept of 'self-therapeutic capacity' will begin to be liberated; all teachers are part of the therapeutic process, either for good or, sadly, for ill.

As we have seen, eventually a gradual clarification of the issue to be faced will emerge: 'So,' the counsellor may reflect, 'you seem to be saying you would like to tackle . . .' When the client accepts such a reflecting comment by the counsellor, it may well be that work at a deeper level is appropriate. This takes us to the second phase, the understanding or insight phase, in which the client is helped to move more deeply into the self, in a way that challengingly permits more demanding exploration.

This phase relies as much as the previous one on the presence of the 'core condition infused' relationship. It accepts that some of the material that is causing difficulties for the client may be well buried, and that, given that it is part of the problem, it will be part of the solution, and so has to be accessed when the client decides it is safe to do so.

We saw in Chapter 6 the demands made of both the client and the counsellor in working with deep material. This aspect of the counsellor's work tries to help the pupil to reduce rigidity in considering the issue to be tackled. The counsellor works to help the client to generate more possibilities, to see the wider frame and develop more perspectives. Thus, towards the end of this phase, the pupil may be able to say something along the lines of, 'I wasn't sure of the issues when we started, and when we clarified them into the key one early on, I wasn't sure of how to tackle it. I felt locked about how I could respond. I now see many more options, and think I need to begin to *choose* what I actually want to do.' This takes us firmly into the action stage of counselling.

So, let's review where we have arrived at: an initial exploratory stage seeks to establish a relationship of sufficient safety between counsellor and pupil that the pupil feels enough trust in the counsellor to begin to engage in some creative risk-taking. This is achieved when the counsellor communicates the core conditions and deploys the skills of attending, reflective listening, accurate reflection of what is heard, paraphrasing and summarizing.

It is essential for the counsellor to work with the pupil's agenda, not his or her own curiosity, interest, expertise, judgement, values. This is how the counsellor conveys to the pupil a sense that he or she is being fully accepted. It is a recognition of the central Rogerian belief in the pupil's 'self-therapeutic capacity': that problem resolution will come from the pupil, not the counsellor. Then, when a full, client-centred exploration has crystallized an issue to be worked on, counsellor and pupil will move on to the deeper levels of the insight or understanding phase. The major general tasks here are:

- to reduce the rigidity which initially characterizes client perceptions of the issue;
- to encourage willingness to work at deeper levels of the person than at the to outset;
- to enhance the stage one moves in the direction of a whole presence in the encounter by moving from material about others to material about the self, moving from talking about past or future issues to talking about 'now' issues and moving from factual disclosure to disclosure of feelings.

The only difference between the demands made of the teacher, tutor, year head or counsellor in this acceptance of the client is that the counsellor will work for longer periods and at greater socio-emotional depth than the others. Rogers

(1983) is adamant that the core conditions for effective therapy are also the core conditions for effective learning. The counsellor (or teacher or tutor or year head) will model the fluidity of perception and comfort with strong emotion that the client is working towards, so that as the rigidity of perception in the client reduces and a greater willingness to explore the full, deep self emerges, the pupil-client will begin to generate a range of possible responses to what had seemed, in the rigid phase, to be an intractable problem. The pupil is now on the edge of action: his or her task is to *operationalize* the exploration and insight gained in the two earlier phases. How do counsellors and teachers help pupils to choose one of several possible options, without taking them over and depriving them of their own rights to decide? And what happens if a pupil, despite all our client-centredness and commitment to her or his autonomy, opts for some course of action that we consider to be harmful?

Adults find it very hard to cede independence to young people – after all, we've been 'there', we know the dangers, we have felt the pain of the mistakes we have made, and would like to protect the young from the same pain. We do fill our school brochures with such laudatory aims as 'to develop in our students the ability to be mature decision-makers', 'to help students grow as mature young adults', 'responsible', yet we fail to see the irony involved in treating them like mental retards and moral reprobates. Both as a parent and as a teacher I am deeply into that paradox. It is probably an inevitable discomfort for both the young and the parent/teacher/mentor, and the initial key to negotiating it with minimum breakdown of mutual respect is to accept that it is there. At its heart lies value dissonance: attitudes to risk, security, love, sexuality, authority, property, violence, wealth, poverty; the list is endless.

Where at one time decision-making was viewed as a *logical* exercise, early work by Gelatt (1962), suggesting that a central decision-making construct is the *value-set* of the decider, has been increasingly influential in the training of leaders and managers in all kinds of organizations. Gelatt does not devalue the cognitive/logical dimension, but he does give it a radically new perspective, particularly in his revisions of the model in 1989. He suggests that when we are faced with a challenge, our initial response is indeed to assemble the richest, most relevant possible data base (see Figure 7.1). We use this information not to decide, but to generate as many feasible options as possible: 'given this information, the *logical possibilities* are . . . *n*'. Once the possibilities are generated as fully as possible, the decider needs to *choose* from among the options. It is at this point that writers on decision-making have begun to see the high significance of values and attitudes when people make their choice. Thus, a counsellor, mentor or adviser needs to help the student to access not only the possibilities, but also what is, in personal terms, the most desirable, valued option. In counselling (or managerial) terms rigid thinking can prevent us seeing all the possibilities, thus reducing our scope for action. The rigidity can have a range of different causes and the effective counsellor needs to develop ways of helping to reduce that pupil narrowness of vision of the possible. A frequent factor is a 'play-safe' tendency, a reluctance to be genuinely creative in case I 'make a fool of myself'. Such attitudes lock us into the conventional, the current dysfunctional situation, the problem being faced. How can we help people to explode into creativity?

The well-tried technique of brainstorming is often used, and too often used badly, to try to enhance fluid, creative thinking. I have watched the fluidity of thinking it is designed to liberate, the creativity and the useful risk-taking crushed as the 'facilitator' censors contributions ('No . . . I think that's a bit over the top'), evaluates them ('Great idea, Tom', then 'Well, Mary, we'll put it down for now') and places them in hierarchies ('I'll put these down in three lists, A, B and C'). The essence of brainstorming is that everything goes down, written haphazardly all over the paper: censorship, evaluation and categorizing come later.

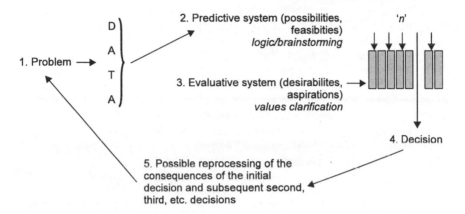

Figure 7.1 Making decisions

I once worked with a group of Youth Training Scheme participants in an area of high unemployment and at a time shortly after the Manpower Services Commission (1982) had circulated all schemes, with the warning that treatment of political or controversial material would lead to the withdrawal of the trainer's grant. The young adults involved had rigidly narrow views of the possibilities for their lives, and I wanted them to throw off the shackles of conventional thinking and to be personally creative. We had spent some time trying to create a supportive, safe group. They numbered 30 and I had them working in five groups of six in a large classroom. So:

'Life is tough. It throws up problems and challenges all the time – about yourself, your family and friends, your work or unemployment, your relationships.' In Gelatt's terms, the problem. 'If you, as small groups, could create some changes that would help you get what you wanted out of life, what would they be? Anything goes; be as wild, inventive as you want, write everything down, don't miss anything out. Let's see who gets the longest list.' In Gelatt's terms, the possibilities. They set to, with a will. I sat still, trying to be as unobtrusive as possible, not wanting to block the initial trickle that grew little by little into a flood: more qualifications (conventional start), stand up for myself more (socio-emotional aims), be more handsome, taller, bigger boobs (adolescent body-image material emerging and testing the boundaries, mine and those of the exercise), get an apprenticeship, win the pools, marry a rich man (followed by one of the lads saying 'marry a rich woman' to general laughter – but no comment, evaluation from me; let it flow), sell my body, become a nurse, a painter and decorator, a mechanic, teacher (roars of laughter from the group, plus 'ye canna even read'), lorry driver, nanny (the vocational self, identified by Wall, 1968, to the fore), win the pools, nick a lot of money (temptation to moralize prematurely and inappropriately resisted). Each of the five groups was unique in its list, but in general they generate similar types of options, and they had moved away from the stultifying, rigid view that they were 'the dole lads and lasses'.

Of course, brainstorming is risky: it might throw up 'material of a political or controversial nature' and lead to the cessation of my grant! Indeed, each of the five groups, using different words but expressing the same sentiment, included an option we can call 'assassinate the prime minister'. Should I have stepped in and said, 'I think that's a bit over the top' or 'I prefer George's option of joining a political party to pursue change'? That I did not do that was not because I approve of violence (I do not), or that I do not see political parties as vehicles of change (I do), it was because I wanted as much creative thinking as I could get, and I wanted to start from where the student/client was. There is much overwhelming evidence that aims that are chosen by the individual are pursued much more committedly than aims that are set or imposed by another person (Cartwright and Zander, 1968; Corey, 1986). What the group was doing was establishing embryonic personal agendas – their own, not mine, and therefore more likely to engage their attention.

Of course, on some occasions the beginning of the 'action phase' will not need to be prefaced with this generation of options. The client, having explored at great depth the nature of a challenge he or she faces, will arrive at the point of being able to respond to a counsellor intervention: 'You seem to be close to saying what it is you would like to do. We've explored, searched, looked to make sense out of things, and I now keep having this feeling that you can see a course of action you would like to pursue.' We could be tempted to be premature, reflecting something that is not there – more my hope than the client's position – and the client will, if we have created a non-directive ambience, be able to say, 'No, not yet, I'm still confused.' And back we go for further exploration. Gelatt sees this as part of the processing of data through the predictive system, helping the client to end up with 'n' feasible objectives.

Let's shift the example from the YTS people. If, after passing through the exploratory phase and the deep insight/understanding phase, the pupil is trying to decide whether to go on to higher education or leave school to look for a job, she or he will be in possession of large quantities of data at both an intellectual and a feeling level: job possibilities, the financial state of the family, the cultural expectations of the family, likely grades for higher education, interest in 'book' learning, sense of responsibility about contributing to a meagre family budget, attitudes about delaying gratification, thoughts about love, relationships, leaving the 'street' and the culture. It cannot be enough for us to intone platitudes about 'a good education' being priceless. It may well be, but the decision-making process needs to involve the person who will benefit or otherwise from the decision. It is sometimes useful at this stage to invite the student to do a 'force field analysis'.

'OK, George. You've really worked hard on this. I think you are saying that out of all the exploring, you now want to decide about whether to stay on and go for a university place. Let me write that down on this large sheet of paper. What I would like you to do is to list on the left-hand side all those factors that seem to lead you in the direction of seeking higher education, and on the right-hand side all those which seem to push against it' (see Figure 7.2).

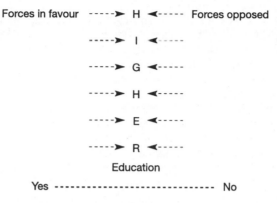

Figure 7.2 Force-field analysis

When the list is completed, the counsellor/teacher will have a *student-generated* decision-making data base, which will contain both cognitive/logical and value/emotional material. After further exploration to ensure that all the issues are on the list, the student should be able to push the issue on which the choice is to be made in the 'yes' or the 'no' direction. While the strategy may seem to be rather clinical on paper, it can have a very liberating effect on thinking and decision-making.

A different approach accepts the recent arguments of Gelatt (1989), Heppner (1989) and de Bono (1990) that much decision-making fails to give enough attention to the 'intuitive' elements which influence our decisions. With university students I have used the following exercise to access intuitive thinking, and to neutralize the conventionality of what de Bono calls 'rock logic'. It involves a relaxation exercise, guided fantasy and decision-making on an intuitive level. It is probably best done in a group, and with gentle music playing in the background. Again, students are enthusiastic about the insights they gain into decision-making.

'Before we begin, can I ask you to draw to mind some issue that is taxing you; something about which you would like to make a decision. Just put it on to a top agenda and let it sit there for the moment. What should I do about it? Can you find a place to stretch out and make yourself as comfortable as possible. You may find it helps to close your eyes . . . allow yourself to become aware of your breathing . . . feel the air entering your nostrils . . . moving coolly down your throat . . . filling your lungs. Enjoy your breathing . . . Now, gently begin to search the outside environment with your listening and find a sound . . . concentrate on it . . . get to know it, sift it . . . after a few moments return to your own body . . . scan it, discover where it feels tense, crushed, uncomfortable and quite deliberately move to ease it, relax, send your relaxing thoughts into the areas of discomfort and, mentally, gently massage them. Check again . . . is your body feeling at ease? . . . the top of your skull, the scalp . . . deliberately relax it. Your eyes, are they tightly shut . . . allow them to ease. Your jaw, are your teeth clenched? Ease them apart. Check your shoulders and neck . . . if they feel tight, clench them hard for three seconds and gradually ease them into the fullest possible relaxation. How is your chest, your tummy, your lower back? . . . check each of them and deliberately allow them to relax. Are your hands and feet without tension . . . your thighs and calves? Scan the whole body again, and luxuriate in the ease you have gained. Relax . . . Now let us go into your imagination. Imagine yourself walking in a leafy wood; you can smell the scent of flowers, hear the birds, the sound of running water and the rustling of small animals. It is cool and comfortable. Sense the wood; as fully as you can. As you are walking, you enter a clearing and can see a small cabin. You have this sudden, deep awareness that inside the cabin is a very wise person, and that you will have one opportunity to ask this person about the issue you put on to your agenda before we begin this exploration. Stay relaxed. Go into the cabin . . . there you see your 'wise adviser'. Simply ask your question and allow the wise person some moments to reply.

'Come out of the cabin back to birdsong, the sound of water, the coolness, and carry the wise answer with you. It does not bind you, you are still the ultimate decision-maker. You can bring the answer back as we return through the wood, back to an awareness of your relaxed body, with its easy, refreshing breathing. Relax . . . and as it feels appropriate, return gently and fully to this room.'

Of course, there is no 'wise person'. Nor would we expect students to base decision-making on some 'intuition' gained in this exercise. Nevertheless, participants do get an answer, and that answer comes not from the guru, but from themselves – some deep values, feelings, insights push them in the direction of 'x' or 'y'. This becomes part of the decision-making data which can challenge the conventional and increase creativity. The material generated should not be simply left. Rather, the student should be helped, in a counselling relationship, to look at the implications and new insights she or he may have gained in the exercise. It is important to add that sometimes the exercise can give students access to troubling material – it is not a game, it is a strategy that helps the student in a non-directed way to find her or his intuitive answer, drawn from deep material, to a challenge in her or his life. In Brammer and Shostrum's terms, it takes decision-making beyond the ego/mastery/logical level to the deeper reaches of feeling, values and attitudes. Frequently, a return to the force field analysis is a beneficial way to process the material generated by the 'wise person' exercise.

It will be clear by now that the 'option-generating and choosing' part of the action stage involves work to accept, clarify and in some way sift all the data that have been produced throughout the counselling process. In the client's own time, the perhaps superficial and initially factual delineation of the issue in the exploratory stage, and the related, buried, denied, covert, minimally-in-the-consciousness material touched and drawn to the surface during the understanding phase, are analysed as a decision-making data base – 'Given all this stuff, what I would really want to do is . . .' – and we have a declaration for action.

Not infrequently clients are able to arrive at such a statement of intent, or at least an aspiration – 'I'd love to . . .' – and then sabotage it by adding, 'but I can't'. The choice is made, but the client undermines it right at the outset. The gestalt therapists, following the dictum of Perls, invite the client to verbalize the perception differently, but more accurately: not 'I can't', rather 'I choose not to'. The 'I'd love to, but I can't' scenario is looked at in the next chapter, where action is the central focus. For the moment we will concentrate on generating possibilities.

We must not set on one side the common anxiety for counsellors and teachers trying to enhance pupil autonomy, which was identified as the second focus in this chapter: how should we respond if, having helped to generate a range of possibilities, the young person opts for one we 'know' is wrong? It is not only the counsellor in school who faces this dilemma – it is a challenge to all counsellors, but in school it is intensified because most of our students are legally minors. The *Code of Ethics* of the British Association for Counselling (1992) can give us an opening purchase on the problem:

> Counsellors should take all reasonable steps to ensure that the client suffers neither physical nor psychological harm during counselling. (2.2.1)

The challenge to the professionalism of the counsellor is of course to determine what is reasonable, and to make judgements about what constitutes in a given case the harm described. It is clear, however, that part of our counsellor role is to protect our client. (Such issues as drug abuse, eating disorders, under-age sexual relationships or other criminal activity could be seen as clearly threatening harm, and meriting a protective as well as a counselling response from the counsellor. A different situation obtains if the perceived harm is the result of judging proposed client actions in the light of our own, perhaps different, value systems. Here such examples as a proposed abortion in a 17-year-old young woman would be totally contrary to the values of, say, a Catholic or a Muslim counsellor.) There is no doubt that from a counselling point of view, if the counsellor is unable to set personal values on one side and to work with the agenda of the client, then she or he should refer the client in a supportive manner to a counsellor who does not face the same dilemma. Clearly, less dramatic value dissonance between client and counsellor can occur, and the same principles would apply. In the absence of danger, the counsellor's task is to work with the phenomenological field of the client.

> Counsellors are responsible for working in ways that promote the client's control over his/her own life, and respect the client's ability to make decisions and change in the light of his/her own beliefs and values. (2.2.3)

In the light of the foregoing comments on the 'minor' status of many of our clients in school, this presents practitioners with a major ethical challenge. We are required both to act protectively when harm threatens, and to respect clients' capacity for decision-making within their own code of values. Obviously there are no clearcut protocols to follow here. We are in the realms of professional judgements which balance client need for safety, clients' right to respect for their own decision-making and counsellor obligations to:

> Be accountable to colleagues, employers and funding bodies as appropriate . . . consistent with responsibilities to the client and the obligation of confidentiality. (B.2.5.1)

The complex balance indicated in this summary of key elements of the ethical code makes it essential that norms, contracts and expectation by both clients and employers are dealt with *proactively*, i.e. we should declare at the outset what our code of practice will be, within the professional code of the BAC and the requirements of the law.

So, not to dodge the initial question, what would I do if I find a client proposing a course of action of which I disapproved? I hope I would decide carefully whether there was danger to the client or others, and if so I would break confidentiality following the guidelines of the Code of Ethics:

> Exceptional circumstances may arise which give the counsellor good grounds for believing that the client will cause serious physical harm to others or themselves . . . in such circumstances the client's consent to a change in the agreement about confidentiality should be sought whenever possible unless there are grounds for believing the client is no longer capable of taking responsibility for their own actions. Whenever possible, the decision to break confidentiality agreed between a counsellor and client should be made only after consultation with a supervisor or experienced counsellor. (B.4.4)

I should check, too, if criminal activity was being proposed, and work with the client on that issue specifically. For me, breaching of confidentiality here would be much more difficult – major drug offences would not meet the same response as limited, personal use of cannabis. However, that clearly comes from my value system, my view of its danger and my view of how I can best help a client.

Finally, if I am aware that my unease is because of a value clash, involving neither danger nor criminality, I should reflect on whether I was capable of setting my values aside to work with the values of the client, partly because I see that as philosophically acceptable to me, but also because I know that I could neither bully nor otherwise inculcate my values into the client. Sutherland and Cooper (1990), analysing stress among workers in the health services, identify the following list of 'basic individual rights':

- the right to make mistakes;
- the right to set one's own priorities;
- the right to have one's own needs considered as important as the needs of other people;
- the right to refuse requests without having to feel guilty;
- the right to express oneself as long as one does not violate the rights of others;
- the right to judge one's own behaviour, thoughts and emotions and to take responsibility for the consequences.

I have children, I teach in schools, I have undergraduate students – and I feel the power of that as a challenge. Letting go of control over the young, granting them freedom to seek their selves, is the hardest task imaginable – but it lies at the heart of each phase of counselling. Rogers's 1942 text puts it most succinctly: 'all the techniques used should aim towards . . . this tendency toward positive, *self-initiated* action' (p. 18).

Before we move on to the action phase, as usual a few exercises are offered to illustrate and exemplify some of the issues just explored.

Exercises

The chapter you have just read is about helping people to choose. It accepts that in order to take a decision, clients need help to see, as fully as possible, what options are available. Some strategies were offered as illustrations in the body of the chapter, but there are many more. An example follows.

No exit

Members of a training group are asked to draw to mind a 'shareable' issue, in which they feel blocked. It is sometimes useful to give a starting focus by suggesting they look at specific areas of their life – work, relationships, identity, some dysfunctional behaviour. Each member of the group is then invited to share the issue to be dealt with, with fellow group members: 'I have this head of department who is always putting me down', or 'My mother-in-law always spoils Christmas, but we have to invite her', or 'I would love to shed 14 pounds but I just have no self-discipline.' Group members usually choose that kind of shareable issue, but occasionally, in a safe, supportive group that has been together for a while, you will get, 'I feel locked into a boring marriage', 'I know my son is doing drugs, and feel powerless to intervene', or other very challenging issues. The declarations are the meat of the exercise.

> *You have each identified an issue that reduces, in some sense, your happiness or effectiveness. It also feels to you like an issue that has blocked you within some kind of cul-de-sac; you see no exit. There is only one option: to get your head down and suffer. This exercise tries to help you to lift the head and look at the real options, rather than the one limited by the stance that says 'I cannot', rather than 'I am choosing not to'. Working with a partner, tell him or her why you are choosing this dysfunctional behaviour. Initially, you may feel that there is no other option, but even if that is the case, it will help to spell out the reasons for that being the single option.*

> *'I choose not to lose weight because . . .' (as many reasons as possible); or*

> *'I am choosing not to confront/face up to my mother-in-law/head of department because . . .'*

> *'I am choosing to stay in an unhappy marriage because . . .'*

> *'I am choosing not to say anything to my son about his drugs because . . .'*

This initial 'explorer' frequently serves to jolt us out of rigidity – it does need the individual to work hard, and the listener to keep the individual on task, without intervening to offer his or her explanations. The exercise is a clear challenge to us that we are not locked, we are choosing.

The second stage, when both members of the pair have had a turn, is to ask the 'magic' question:

> *You have cited all the reasons for choosing your current course of action, which you say is in some way a painful course of action for you. If you could wave a magic wand, tell your partner what you would ideally like to happen. Be as precise as you can.*

'I would stop eating "x" or "y".'

'I would face up to my mother-in-law/head of department and tell her or him.'

'I would talk to my partner about my unhappiness, and suggest we go to Relate.'

'I would ask my son if we could have a talk about my fears.'

OK, if everyone has had a go at waving the magic wand, take turns to identify what is stopping you from taking the course of action you say you would like to take. You have a clear, preferred option, but you are choosing not to adopt it.

The intention of the exercise is not to bully people into some action they may not want to take. It is to loosen that stultifying rigidity that frequently reduces our effectiveness – habit, fears, anxieties, a desire for 'the easy option' even though it leaves us unhappy, a hope that the problem will just go away. We will, using this approach or a variation on it, expand our perception of the possible, identify our preferred scenario and set the scene for the action phase, which we look at in the next chapter.

CHAPTER 8

Action

In Chapter 7 careful attention was paid to a common human experience – that of feeling driven by circumstances beyond our control to a course of action that we would prefer not to take. While we can all probably identify with the feelings of inadequacy that leave us saying, 'I'd love to but I can't', even a brief consideration leaves us challenged by Perls's contention that it is not so much that I can't, rather that I have chosen not to. The astonishing paradox is that too often the implicit, unexamined choice is for something we do not want. There is a rather ghoulish joke in the medical fraternity that has a physician saying, 'Show me a healthy person, and I will show you someone who has been inadequately investigated.' We could adapt that to dysfunctional behaviour and say, 'Show me someone who is choosing to be unhappy, and I will show you someone whose decision-making has been inadequately investigated.'

We ended Chapter 7 with clients exploring choices and being helped to come, via a challenging and supportive process, to a statement of their preferred course of action: 'Of all the possibilities open to me, the one I would like to do is . . .' This chapter examines the 'how' of the journey from declaration of intent to implementation of that intent. The decisions we take are myriad, and so it is inevitable that one example will miss the nuances of the numerous others not chosen. Nevertheless, it is probably most effective to use examples to illustrate the processes involved in making the move from opting to acting. In the previous chapter, by way of illustration of the kinds of options individuals identify as desirable, we talked about weight loss, confrontation with difficult work colleagues or family members and so on. In school too the range will be enormous: changes in personal behaviour (truancy, disruption, bullying), styles of relating, work patterns, decisions about vocational and higher education issues, questions about burgeoning sexuality and so on. Sometimes after the exploration, the deep understanding, the option generation and selection have been completed, the client needs no further help from the counsellor. More frequently, however, the 'I want to do this but I can't' syndrome leaves the counsellor with one further area of helping: the construction, implementation and evaluation of an action plan.

The client still needs to experience this part of the counselling process as infused by the core conditions. The temptation for the counsellor is to be impatient, to sniff the water hole in the desert and start galloping towards it – to take over the client. As at each stage analysed so far, it is crucial that the process, the agenda, the direction and the pace of progress stay with the client. Some key stages remain to be negotiated.

In seeking to implement the daunting, 'I can't' decision, the student will be helped as follows:

- the skills of action planning;
- contracting;
- role-playing hoped-for actions in the safety of the counselling encounter;
- having the counsellor model difficult, desired behaviour;
- monitoring the outcomes of implementing the desired behaviour;
- evaluating how successful the determined action has been.

ACTION PLANNING

It is important to help the student to identify small, genuinely feasible steps towards the desired action. The 'I can't' starting-point can be the result of the student's perception of the change as so enormous as to be impossible to contemplate; setting out this series of steps can bring the desired ultimate action within the bounds of possibility. Let's go through the process with Ruth, 14 years old and a known school bully. Although this choice narrows us to a specific case, readers will see how the general shape of responding is applicable to a wide range of pupil behaviours.

Ruth will have gone through the phases of counselling analysed in detail in the previous chapters – we will presume that a referral by a member of staff has been skilfully shifted to a 'self-referral' by the teacher-counsellor or counsellor, ensuring that the counselling is not done 'to' Ruth, but with her. After a supportive and challenging journey through the exploratory and insight phases of counselling, we will presume that Ruth has 'told her story' and gained deep insight into it during the understanding phase of her work with the counsellor, looking at her values, the attitudes from which her behaviour springs, the deep personal material which explodes out of her periodically in cruelty to others – all of this work done in an atmosphere of such safety that she is willing to contemplate a radical shift in her behaviour. 'Yeah, I know it's stupid and hurts Mandy [her principal victim], and I wish I could stop. but it's, like, automatic. I don't think "I'm going to make Mandy cry" – the others push me to it.' I wish I could stop; there is the meat of the action plan.

Ruth needs to have that reflected to her, supportively, but also as a challenge: 'I am trying to understand what you mean when you say, "I want to stop" and in the next breath, "but I can't". You always strike me as someone who does what she wants to do, but in this case you're telling me there is something or things that get in the way of you doing what you want. Can we have a look at the blocks in more detail? Let's really have a good look at the things that stop you doing what you want to do.'

It would be possible to follow this up verbally, listening, reflecting, summarizing and looking at patterns and themes. An alternative would be to use visual material. Students often find the activity of drawing, painting or constructing other visual stimuli a liberating experience. The pursuit of a conversation can push the client into the realms of logic and cognition at a moment when the elements which drive her actions, or failure to act, are socio-emotional. Drawing gives access to what have been called 'the client's internal landscapes' – it permits a projection of influential internal material outside, so that counsellor and client can peruse, work on and own the material. Invisible blocks to action become visible, blocks not drawn into the action plan become part of the analysis (Figure 8.1).

'So, Ruth. You want to stop your bullying, but it seems there are some obstacles that stop you. Can we try something to get inside what those blocks are? Would you, on this sheet of paper, draw the Ruth who bullies – towards the centre of the page, but a little to the left-hand side. That's the "now" Ruth, but not the one you want to be. What is she like? How does she look? Now draw a line from the now Ruth to the Ruth you'd like to be (Figure 8.2), and draw a "new" Ruth. What is she like? How would it feel to be her?'

The client needs a large sheet of paper, encouragement that you don't have to be a good drawer (most children enjoy drawing even if they are not) and time to explore and commit the 'externalizing' of the exploration to paper. At the end of this part of the exercise, the counsellor and Ruth will have some rich insights into the two ways of being Ruth. This can be processed in the same way we would process any disclosures in a counselling encounter, accurately reflecting what has been shared on the paper, checking that the externalization matches the verbalizing at the opening of the encounter. If there is a mismatch, then we will need to go back to the option selection stage discussed earlier. Let us presume that Ruth does depict her two selves in a way that permits the reflection: 'I must say the "now" Ruth looks a bit fierce. I wouldn't like to meet her in an alley on a dark night! Can you see any difference between her and the "new" Ruth? Which do you prefer? What is attractive about the fierce you . . . the new you?'

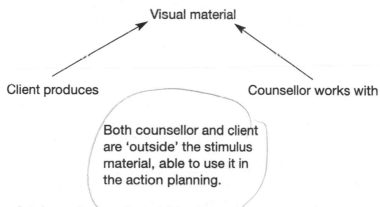

Figure 8.1 Accessing our 'internal landscapes'

now Ruth ------------> Ruth who doesn't bully

Pull me back   Help me forward

Figure 8.2 Visualizing a behavioural shift

The encounter would continue, exploring and clarifying that 'I don't want to be a bully' is a true representation of where Ruth has got to. Probably, the client will get hold of some good experiences of the bully mode – enjoying being in control, power, strength – and the counsellor will need to work carefully with that, helping the client to separate 'my' power, strength and control from cruelty, insensitivity and the freedom of others. This, of course, will be done in a counselling context, not with some power play by the counsellor using superior logic and argumentation. Ruth will be most likely to change if she sets the objectives and controls the process of change.

'OK, Ruth. So the "new" you seems attractive, but you still have this "I can't change" feeling. Can I ask you to go back to your drawing and to draw in or write in all the things that are pulling you back from change – anything you can think of at all. Then those things that help you move towards being the Ruth you would like to be.' (As I write this, I feel the contrast between the ease with which the process can be written down and the meticulous counsellor care which is needed to facilitate the generation of the material. It reminds me of the Norcross and Guy (1989) caveat to counsellors to avoid the tyranny of technique and to maintain constant awareness of the centrality of the relationship in effective counselling. That is no less true when we are operating in the action phase.)

By now Ruth will be identifying people, events, times and emotions that either block or facilitate her desired change – and the time to invite her to specify actions has come. Another matrix can help her (Figure 8.3)

- to put herself at the centre of the process;
- to identify key influences on her desired behaviour;
- to stipulate small, cumulative, feasible steps towards the desired behaviour;
- to emphasize *actions*.

Time scale	tomorrow	next week	next month	next year	sometime
RUTH					
Friends, peers					
Teachers					
Family					
Places					
Occasions					
Other influences					

Figure 8.3 Action planning

The client is invited and helped to declare actions that will be taken, a time scale on which they will be taken, the person with whom the action will need to be taken and sometimes the arena where the action will be taken. This simply recognizes the great complexity of any decision we wish to take: on whom will it have impact besides me, what will that person's reaction be, how can I enhance those who are helpful to my cause or reduce the impact of those who will hinder or sabotage me? The boxes of the matrix will use the material from Figure 8.2, as well as any other issues Ruth would want to put in.

Given this new analytical data base, Ruth can go through key material, crucially generated by her, cell by cell, making a series of small contracts with herself – and by implication with her counsellor. It is a declaration of intent:

Friends/peers: today
When I leave this session, I will tell Debbie that we're going to leave Mandy alone.

Friends/peers: next week
I am going to ask Mandy if she wants to come skating with us.

Teachers: next week
I will tell Mr Haslett (year tutor who had first responded to bullying to protect Mandy) that we have had some sessions and explain what I want to do.

Places: today, next week, next month
I am going to stop going to the pine trees (edge of the playing fields).

Again, to write things down in this way suggests that this is a straightforward process – of course, it is slow and painstaking, but it does offer clear objectives, set by the client, which can be used to monitor progress.

CONTRACTING

Until the client has engaged in the detailed analysis suggested above – or some similar attempt to operationalize hopes and wishes – the precision of a contract is not possible. Students are well aware of the seriousness of a contract, and feel doubly committed if they 'run' the formulation of it. Nelson-Jones (1982) describes contracting as the 'bridge' between the exploratory work and the formulation of working goals. He adds, 'it is important that the summarization statement is clear and checked with clients for accuracy and adequate coverage of their major concerns' (p. 283). His caveat that the counsellor must also check that the client is prepared to proceed with the declared working goals is a realistic one. He says that if the answer is yes, then a 'contract' is in operation; if no, then further clarification will be necessary, going as far back as need be into the stages of the counselling process.

ROLE-PLAYING

For Ruth to tell Debbie that their baiting of Mandy is over is an enormously demanding task. In counselling, it is not infrequently the case that a desired outcome (I will apologize to . . .) is more easily said than done. With a group of teachers who were doing an MA in counselling I once talked about an argument I had had with my teenage son. It had become acrimonious – my fault – and we had parted on very bad terms. I knew that I dished out to him a load of bad temper and aggression that had been churned up in work, and did not belong to him – but he had received it. Like, I think, many people, I find it very hard to apologize – particularly when I am wrong! I could explore this mini-incident in my domestic life, analyse it, even touch deep material about authority, self-esteem and oedipal complexes. I knew I was wrong; could say I want to apologize, 'but I can't'. In fact I was choosing not to. The group suggested I role-played the apology – one of them agreed to act the part of my son, as I tested out a scenario. 'Can I have a word, John.' (The group said that sounded ominous.) Try again. 'Hi John! Good day? Oh about this morning, sorry about that. I think I went a bit over the top. Pals?' (They thought this was better, felt it was a bit manipulative in that the opening was a blind, and demeaning when I said 'Oh,' suggesting, 'I just remembered this insignificant little thing' – a 'bit' over the top.) The simple activity of testing ways of carrying out my action continued to develop my insight into the incident. The mental rehearsal had the effect of allowing me to practise a challenging new behaviour, and the responses of the group, my 'counsellor', allowed me to explore the 'what will happen if I do it this way' question. Clients often fantasize about the disastrous consequences that will flow from their intended action; role-playing is a helpful way to challenge the fantasy. I fantasized that I would be humiliated by saying 'sorry', that my son would say 'get lost' or worse, so I wove protectors around my apology to anticipate the 'disaster'. I still had not got to the way I wanted to do it. Like many clients, I needed further help from my counsellor.

Sometimes the client will arrive at a comfortable way of doing what she or he wants to by following the strategy described above. She or he role-plays it, it feels effective, the feedback from the counsellor permits her or him to be more confident about testing the behaviour in a real situation. When there are still feelings of awkwardness, a further strategy is available to the client and counsellor.

MODELLING

Despite the rather jargoned way of saying it, Nelson-Jones (1982) reminds us of an important insight of the social learning theorist, Bandura. 'Bandura', he says, 'considers modelling . . . to be the principal mode of transmitting new modes of behaviour' (p. 135). This is one explanation of the importance of the relationship in counselling as the major influence on therapeutic movement. The effective counsellor 'models' highly functional behaviour, i.e. behaviour which is respectful to the client, cognizant of the intrinsic – not merely consequential – dignity of the client, open to the expression of emotion, honest and genuine. The client observes this style of behaving and sees it as a real possibility, not an unattainable ideal – 'I have seen it done!' This, however, operates at the level of the general. To model specificities also has a powerful potential for the hesitant client. To return to my apology, the group asked me to be my son, while one of them modelled for me their view of a genuine action, drawn from the data I had shared. The 'model' said to me, 'John, I'm really sorry about being such a pain this morning; it had nothing to do with you; I was just bunging bad temper from work on to whoever I bumped into first. It was unforgiveable.' I wasn't sure how my son would react that that. It seemed 'clean' as a statement, with no hidden bits. But I didn't feel too happy with the 'it was unforgiveable' bit. We negotiated, and I changed it (it had to be my action) to 'I should never have behaved like that. I am very sorry.' So, via roleplay and modelling, I had arrived at *specifically* what I would do. We will return to that in a moment.

Clearly the tasks before Ruth are more complex, but the process is the same. Specific actions, with specific people, at specific times and in specific locations, are generated and then run through the same process. She can be helped to fantasize about the disaster that might occur in her conversation with Debbie (rejection, aggression) and her form tutor (disbelief, humiliation) by role-playing what she might do and how. If that is not sufficient, then the counsellor can model behaviours for her. This is not easy, and it needs creative planning before and negotiation during the modelling, so that at the end of the process Ruth has her own action, not an imposed one.

MONITORING

When the action phase is the end point of a long and complex series of counselling sessions, and consists of a series of actions planned to take place sequentially over a period of time, an important support for the client will be regular sessions to monitor progress and, if necessary, to revise the plan. The monitoring sessions need to be very specific in their analysis of the extent to which actions have been taken as contracted. It may be that new problems have emerged that are the result of the action taken, and this would involve the counselling following the circularity indicated in the Gelatt model in Figure 7.1, returning to the initial stage of the decision-making model. A further benefit of the monitoring dimension is that new behaviour is challenging, and clients need support in its early stages. If they are pushed out to sea, to fend for themselves, the likelihood is that they will soon be back in our offices, with a reinforced view that their new behaviour cannot be done. The monitoring activity supports, refines and reinforces positively the new behaviours sought by the client.

EVALUATION

There will be a final session! Little by little the client will begin to own fully the new behaviours. Early discomforts will ease and the benefits of a *personally* selected new style of being will be enjoyed. Progress may sometimes feel slow, but it will occur. It is the client who evaluates – I as counsellor may have my view, but the person who can declare 'This is valuable to me in my life' must be the client. So, back to my apology. I returned home that evening. I was delighted to find the girls out (what a coward!), and my wife still at work. I had been getting word perfect in the car, and was surprised at how nervous I was. 'John, I'm really sorry about being such a pain this morning. It had nothing to do with you. I was just bunging bad temper from work onto whoever I bumped into first. I should never have behaved like that. I am very sorry.' Practice had made perfect. He looked at me briefly, turned and walked out of the room. My heart sank – disaster, back to the drawing board. At least I had apologized, but apparently to little effect. I flopped wearily onto the sofa. Five minutes later I was astonished as the recipient of my apology arrived with a tray, a cup of tea and a ham sandwich for me. He put it on an occasional table, smiled and walked out. The olive branch – yes, pals.

It is not always like that. How could it be? We have spent several chapters coming to terms with just how much baggage we all carry around with us in unexamined knapsacks: students, teachers, parents, all struggling to make sense of material that bubbles up unannounced, unexpected and often unwanted; and having made sense of it, to respond to it via an ongoing action plan we call life.

Egan (1986) ends his presentation of a 'model' of counselling by describing his model as 'rational, linear, and systematic', and then wisely anticipates the objection of readers that life is often non-linear, irrational and chaotic. I am sure that teachers will feel that young people have black belts in non-linear, irrational and chaotic responses to life. Perhaps we all do, and that is what makes life interesting. That said, models, structures, grand designs must be seen as essentially flawed – they cannot be sufficiently robust, strong, subtle to cope with the unpredictability of life. What they can do is be the same as a rather rocky, slippery river bed, on which we plant rather apprehensive feet as we try to make sense of the torrent that rushes past our thighs. They are imperfect, but they do offer the possibility of navigational points, resting points, opportunities for getting our bearings. That is the spirit in which my journey has been offered.

Exercises

Several exercises have been described within the chapter, and it seems appropriate at this point to focus on ourselves here, rather than on our pupils. The following activity is designed to help us as counsellors/teachers to empathize

with the blocked feeling clients often express in their 'I want to . . . but I can't'
phase.

We will imagine that the earlier explorations have been done, and that 'the
issue' has emerged.

> *Few of us feel our life is perfect, and we rarely have the time to reflect
> on the blemishes that reduce its perfection. Spend a few moments of
> reflection to identify one issue, over which you have control, that could
> be changed to improve your life. Divorce? Marriage? Religious
> commitment? Participation in sport? Weight loss? Reduced drinking,
> smoking? Quitting altogether? Reading more? Going to the opera?
> Getting a season ticket for Newcastle United . . . The list is endless,
> ranging from the seriously serious to items that appear to be almost
> facetious. Choose one you feel comfortable about giving a good workout.*

> - *How would this improve your life? Be specific; make a list
>   (brainstorm). Invite a counsellor-colleague to help you explore the
>   benefits, and each of the following tasks. Take turns as client and
>   counsellor.*
> - *Given the beneficial potential of this change, what is blocking you
>   from doing it? Does this list reduce the attractiveness of the change?*
> - *Are there any factors that would help or facilitate the change? Can
>   they be harnessed in some way?*
> - *Do you still see the change as facilitative of an improved lifestyle?
>   If so, identify one action you could take tomorrow that would help
>   to achieve the change, and operationalize it. Make a plan and if
>   appropriate role-play or ask a colleague to model it.*
> - *Make a personal contract and agree a monitoring or evaluation
>   session with your colleague.*
> - *When that occurs, do a serious, careful analysis of the extent to
>   which you have managed to keep to the contract. If you have done
>   well, reinforce your success. If for whatever reason you have not kept
>   to the contract that you formulated, go back to Gelatt or the force
>   field analysis to discover why. You may wish to revise your contract,
>   take up a new one or conclude, like me, that your failure to devise
>   a more enhancing lifestyle is due to serious character defects that
>   are probably genetic!*

We need to keep a sense of humour in counselling, and that does not imply a
lack of commitment or seriousness in our counselling endeavours. It is a
recognition of the reality of the human condition, that human beings have a highly
developed capacity to screw up the most carefully devised plans and models. In
the final analysis, the counsellor is there to help the client choose effectively a
lifestyle which is based on the fullest available data, processed both logically and
socio-emotionally. That help must be client-centred.

CHAPTER 9

Special isssues for the counsellor in school

It is useful to remind ourselves at this point that teachers, who may not have the responsibility, the time, the expertise or the inclination to engage in counselling, are the key personnel in school. Further, it is undoubtedly the case that both teachers and school counsellors engage in helping activities with pupils who face socio-emotional challenges beyond the normal academic focus of the school, and each does so in accord with her or his expertise and responsibility. The foregoing chapters have explored the intense demands of that professional activity, whether by teachers or specialist counsellors, and it may be opportune at this point to look in more detail at the differences in responsibility and activity of different members of the school's staff.

Hamblin, in both his 1974 pioneering text and the more recent, 1993, update of the original work on teachers and counselling, speaks of three 'levels of counselling': the immediate level, the intermediate level and the intensive level. He sees the first level as being concerned with promoting a 'positive climate for learning'. It involves all teachers in creating the respecting 'counselling relationship', on which so much emphasis has been placed in this text, and deploying basic counselling skills in a way that enhances the performance of pupils. It involves us all, too, in first-line identification of pupils in difficulties and skilful referrals to colleagues with the time, responsibility and training to respond to referrals. A key performance indicator for a pastoral care system is its capacity for individualizing pupils – there should be no needles in haystacks, and the task of individualizing every pupil in the school is a task of the immediate counselling skills of the classroom teacher. The intermediate level of counselling is where the first counselling *per se* takes place – teachers who have training as counsellors and who have been designated by the school as referral points, properly resourced in time and accommodation to work not only with troubled pupils, but also in a developmental way with all pupils. Schools ought to take a careful inventory of the availability, development and the use of such expertise. The more schools have teachers with these skills, the less will be the need for access to the intensive level of counselling. This will occur with those pupils whose difficulties require time and expertise of a specialist nature – an ability to work with the 'core material' discussed in Chapter 6. Some schools will have such expertise on their staff, others will have to make referrals outside the school. It is important to stress that the *role* of a staff member is not the key factor in assessing and planning counselling provision. Sometimes a form tutor will be more highly trained in counselling than a pastoral or deputy head. The key managerial task for the headteacher is to assign specialist counselling tasks to well-trained counsellors.

Figure 9.1 identifies some general structural elements on this issue. It inevitably oversimplifies, but it does signal clearly that the provision of counselling for pupils is not the work of an isolated individual. This is as much a team effort as any other activity of the school.

	Academic	Socio-emotional	Counselling
Class teacher	National Curriculum cognitive development exams	pupil esteem support challenge	core conditions listening referral
Middle manager	as above and overview standards	as above and records ethics	first-line counselling awareness of limits of expertise/time
Counsellor	liaise with academic specialists	case conference (confidentiality) monitor school ethos	full range of counselling skills referral possibilities

Figure 9.1 Responsibility focus

However, in addition to the detail of the counselling process and the relationships within which it occurs, there are a number of general comments which it seems useful to make on some of the special issues frequently raised by teachers about this area of their work – comments that have significance for both teachers and counsellors. This chapter will try to identify some of these broad, strategic issues, which influence the way in which our young people will tackle special challenges.

The 'special issues' identified below are no more than my effort to respond to professional development day queries that are made on a regular basis. It is not that some pupil difficulties have an importance that others do not – the phenomenological base of counselling will always leave us accepting the pupils' view of the relative importance of different issues. Hufton (1986), for example, in her survey of secondary school students' experience of 'loss', was almost amused to find that the loss of favourite toys, distant uncles or pets was reported alongside of and with no discrimination from the death of parents and siblings – but for the counsellor, if it is hurting the child, then it is material for a counselling response. A similar survey by Carey (1993) found that teachers listed 77 different kinds of potential 'life crises' for pupils. Again, they included a range (I note that my evaluative inclination turns the 'list' unjustly into a 'range' that reflects my assessment of seriousness, not the pupils') that ran from the apparently less demanding challenges of pet death or failure to meet expectations, through eviction, parental redundancy and debt, on to abuse, death in the family and disasters. These were issues drawn from the experience of teachers, and within that list lies the explanation for much pupil underachievement and unhappiness. It can also alert us to the need to develop the kind of pastoral sensitivity in schools that the model produced by Carey would permit. The task of identifying those making 'cries for help' involves the presence of highly sophisticated pastoral care systems (McGuiness, 1989; Carey, 1993) that so individualize pupils that the detection of cries for help is greatly enhanced. The task of responding to those cries for help is the work of the counsellors and teacher-counsellors to whom this book is primarily addressed.

It has been argued, though less vociferously today than in the recent past, that though the surveys mentioned above may be accurate indicators of pupil need, they are not identifying a need that schools should be involved in supplying. These needs, it is argued, are the responsibility of social workers, general practitioners or other medical, psychological and social services. This 'ostrich position' is a stance that is increasingly challenged by work such as Bishop's (1990) survey of the adolescent's view and Harris's (1996) analysis of pupils' wants (they would like a counselling provision in school), Moore *et al.*'s (1996) analysis of a school perspective (teachers too see the need) and McGuiness's (1992) paper analysing the extent to which large employers are taking on board the significant impact on performance of the socio-emotional state of employees, and the employment of counsellors to develop that part of their 'health and safety' provision. Very powerful arguments, drawn from the teachers in the field, from empirical research in psychology and from examinations of cognate activities in business and commerce, suggest that not to have available counselling provision for our pupils is to treat them less favourably than their parents working in large multinational companies. Work I have done with large companies makes it clear that their personnel departments are deeply aware of the importance of psychological health in the workplace – and that they *plan* contingency as well as actual responses.

Carey's (1993) list of 77 potential life crises in the school lives of pupils obliges me to categorize the examples into broad types. There is a real sense in which a counsellor can say, 'counselling is counselling is counselling . . . there are no special issues'. What *is* a variable is the impact that different issues have on the counsellor. If my comfort with my own sexuality is low and unexamined, I will not do sex education or sexual abuse counselling well; if I have unresolved pain related to a bereavement, then I need to work on that before I sit close to the pain of a bereaved child; if my own age and illness have rendered me apprehensive about death, then my guarded thinking will not be helpful to a client who has seen, say, a fatal road traffic accident. That is not to say that *my* hurts and anxieties stop me being human with others who are hurting or anxious, but they will prevent me working at depth as a counsellor with them. Once more, we come to the obligation on counsellors to justify approaching the pain of others by having previously approached their own pain – seeking to come to terms with the problematic in themselves. So, at the risk of oversimplification, I will look at three main areas of 'life crises': traumatized children, children in transition and children in trouble.

TRAUMATIZED CHILDREN

Disasters

It is sadly increasingly the case that a whole school will have to respond to a tragedy that has befallen one or more members of its community. Alongside the incidents that become national news – the fatal stabbing of a young woman in a Cleveland school, the mass murder of children and their teacher at Dunblane Primary School in Scotland or the machete attack on nursery pupils in the Midlands – there are road traffic accidents, accidental deaths, staff and pupil suicides, which reach down to touch the deepest terrors of the entire school community. Such incidents can have a devastating effect at every level, on every activity and each person associated with the school – there is literally no way in which a school can avoid being caught up in the aftermath of such events. Skilled, trained counsellors, using the skills delineated in this book, can make a therapeutic response, but they will need to make it within a whole-school framework.

An outstanding aid to schools in responding to these demands is the succinct and action-focused work of Yule and Gold (1993). This seems to me to be an invaluable planning document for pastoral staff, those responsible for counselling and school governors. They present four key steps, drawn from a document of the New South Wales Schools' Department, which all schools ought to take:

- identify potential critical incidents;
- identify support agencies and personnel;
- have a 'school critical incident management plan';
- have a documented list of roles and tasks for all staff.

I cannot overemphasize the obligation on schools to prepare, organizationally, in this way. The meticulous detail of the Yule and Gold book merits the careful attention of managers – our task in this text is to look at some of the interpersonal issues. This different, more interpersonal perspective is excellently offered in Leaman's (1995) work on the impact of death and loss on children.

Somewhat technically, victims of the kind of incidents which would emerge from the exploration of the first item on the list will be experiencing 'post-trauma distress syndrome'. It is a syndrome described in the *Diagnostic and Statistical Manual of Mental Disorders* (American Psychiatric Association, 1980) as having five key dimensions:

- the client must have witnessed or experienced a serious threat to life or well-being;
- the client must have re-experienced the event in some way (flashbacks, dreams, panic attacks and, in young children, trauma-specific re-enactment);
- the client must consistently avoid stimuli associated with the trauma, or feel a numbing of responsiveness;
- the client must experience persistent symptoms of increased arousal (irritability, flashes of anger, hypervigilance, exaggerated sense of danger, sleeping problems, difficulty in concentrating);
- the symptoms must last at least a month.

While at one level it is clear that a specialist response to those most severely affected is needed, all teachers need to be aware of the likely symptoms of the syndrome. The counselling process finds theoretical roots in the work of Brammer and Shostrum described in Chapter 6: helping the client, in a safe environment, and at his or her own pace, to approach the memory of the trauma which is initially consigned to the deep core, 'safely' held inside the inner defence system. All of the challenges outlined in Chapter 5 face the counsellor working in this area. Teachers who are not in a counselling relationship with the pupil nevertheless need to be extremely sensitive to the challenging material the pupil is carrying around; she or he may officially be doing maths or French, but alongside the academic work, a desperate struggle not to be overwhelmed by the experience is going on.

Herman (1992) makes this salutary comment: 'The core experiences of psychological trauma are disempowerment and disconnection from others. Recovery therefore is based on the empowerment of the survivor and the creation of new connections . . . Recovery can only take place within the context of relationships' (p. 133). She goes on to identify a number of characteristics that need to be reshaped, re-established; they must have a priority over all other learning. Herman describes them as basic capacities: trust, autonomy, initiative, competence, identity and intimacy; the list could be taken from Rogers's (1982) writing on learning and counselling. From the school's point of view, the requirement to help recovery to take place in the context of relationships should be met by current, pre-disaster characteristics of the school; the demands are the same as would be made of any school with a facilitative ethos. An audit, using the disaster scenario as a benchmark, would be a courageous and professional thing to do.

Responses

The debate on the best way to respond to the child traumatized in physical, sexual or psychological abuse approaches the challenge in two ways: preventive measures (e.g. Elliott, 1990) and response measures (e.g. Courtois, 1988; Maher, 1990). The setting up of programmes like the 1986 Kidscape curricular material, designed to help children prevent abuse happening to them, has been criticized (Adams, 1990) on the grounds that it implies a control of the situation which children do not have, and a consequent capacity for self-blame when/if it does occur. Elliott acknowledges the possibility but comes down strongly in favour of the self-esteem and assertiveness skills involved in helping children to say 'no'. My view is that, having acknowledged the possibility that preventive approaches may have unintended effects, careful use of the material will reduce the likelihood of those effects occurring. It seems entirely appropriate to me to develop in schools both the preventive and the general response strategies outlined in the three papers mentioned. The concern of this text is the stage which follows the identification of the child in difficulties. Where am I, whether as counsellor or teacher, on the key issues of power, authority, sexuality, violence and trust? I recently worked with a group of counsellors, some of whom were teachers, on case material of children's descriptions of the experience of abuse. It was deliberately harrowing material, and the session was called 'Incest: If you think the word is ugly . . .' The processing of the experience by the group included comments like:

'I was enraged at the perpetrators'

'I was fearful of the gory detail, it upset me deeply'

'I felt like a voyeur'

'I feel exhausted'

'I never realized the demands disclosure makes on the client – it hurts'

'I am exhausted'

'I felt very sensitized to my own sexual attitudes'

The structures to prevent and detect abuse need to be there. There is no better literature for teachers on that than the papers in the journal *Pastoral Care in Education* (see appendix), but in the final analysis, having helped sufferers to disclose, we need to be able to help them to survive – and eventually prosper. This takes us firmly into the counselling encounter (see Chapter 5).

CHILDREN IN TRANSITION

Chapter 4 considered the pervasiveness of change in modern life, and, in general terms, a second category which merits consideration is that of pupils facing the challenge of change. The changes our pupils are asked to cope with include 'normal' changes like changing schools (or even groups within the school), the traumatic transitions of bereavement (which have useful theoretical inputs from the previous section) and the developmental changes of adolescence, and moving from school to higher education or the world of work (or non-work). Such changes make severe demands on the coping strategies of pupils, and both teachers and counsellors will find themselves involved in responding to pupils' stress. A useful way into the concept is our own reaction to the changes which we face as adults: marriage, separation, divorce, job change, house change, redundancy and so on. By analysing our own reactions we can get some general perception of the process that our pupils face.

Adams (1976) offered a general model of transition which maps the typical phases that allow us to negotiate a change. A significant part of the challenge of change is the impact that it has on our self-esteem, and we can use an esteem axis and a time axis to develop Adams's model (Figure 9.2). The reaction of children tends to be more chaotic, less predictable than that suggested in Adams's model. Nevertheless, the model does present us with some helpful contructs in understanding transition.

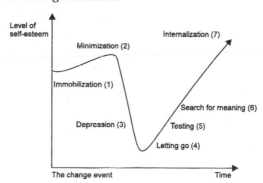

Figure 9.2 Responding to change

Adams would not suggest that this pattern is inevitable or precisely predictable in its duration or sequentiality, but it is based on clinical experience and matches to a greater or lesser extent commonly felt elements in the change experience. Having to hand such a model can be reassuring, both to the counsellor and to the person experiencing severe change:

1. *Immobilization*. Immediately after the precipitating event occurs, individuals will frequently shut off in a self-protective way – banishing the potentially destructive awareness to the core. Pushing, urging the victim to 'face' the reality, is clearly not counselling; creating the kind of safe ambience which encourages the client to begin to accept that the 'event' has occurred is the task. The length of time that a victim requires to take that first courageous step varies enormously.

2. *Minimization*. Once the client is able to look the change in the face, the reality can still be such that it needs to be distorted, so this stage is characterized by a tendency to be unrealistically optimistic or to accept the basic reality while denying the unpleasant consequences. These staged acceptances of the truth are the normal healthy reaction to major transition events. The client is working towards grappling with the challenge, but will do so at her or his own pace. Careful, supportive listening and accurate reflection will make it more possible for the client to approach the reality of the event. When that full grasping of the reality occurs then a frequent response is depression.

3. *Depression*. This lowering of expectations in the face of the unvarnished reality of the situation can be accompanied by profound emotions – anger, despair, helplessness, hopelessness, hatred – and a range of dysfunctional behaviours – lashing out, swearing, verbal aggression. 'Nothing is worth a candle', life has 'no purpose'. The task of the counsellor is not to offer false reassurances, to soothe, to deflect the client from the reality of the pain, but simply to be there, reflecting accurately, picking up themes, allowing the client to stand – with support – in the depths of despair. 'At the moment, you can see no glimmer of optimism, no reason for hope' (accurate reflection), and 'I think I'd like to say that I and lots of other people are going to stand by you hoping that that will change' (genuineness and an attempt to touch whatever glimmers of hope lie in the depths of the client's misery; see Chapter 5).

4. *Letting go*. The first three stages are the consequence of attachment to the past, the pre-change time. That past is familiar, known, secure and the habitual locus of safety. Now the client detaches himself from the past, lets go of those securities and what has been, recognizing their value, but also seeing that they are no more, except as memories and springboards to what is new. There is an acknowledgement and anticipation of a different future, with the new possibilities that might hold. This is a courageous step to take.

5. *Testing*. As the client emerges from attachment to the past and begins to accept that a new future is to be faced, a range of new coping skills emerge, testing out the new reality. This can be a time of frustration, anger and disappointment as well as growing energy and activity.

6. *Search for meaning*. The characteristic 'life has lost its meaning' phase of the despair stage is now challenged. The client is using the new

experiences to construct new perceptions and values. The transition event is now placed firmly in the past, less threatening, no longer devastating, though still capable of stirring painful re-experiencing of the pre-change time.

7. *Internalization*. This begins to occur as the individual is able to experience the transition and incorporate it into a new meaning of her or his world. She or he enjoys the sensation of coping and mastery, and develops growing self-esteem in the knowledge that she or he has 'made sense' of the senseless and emerged whole from the process.

Excellent detailed work on the specifics of school response in these areas can be found in Eiser *et al*. (1995), who examine teacher attitudes towards placing death and bereavement issues within the curriculum, Wells (1988), who looks at how children who are bereaved might be responded to, Leaman (1995), who provides deep insight into children's perceptions of death and loss, and Ward and associates (1988/9), whose *Good Grief* focuses on the move towards stage 7 in the list above. Sexual changes and our ability to respond to them are sensitively and sensibly treated in two papers published by NAPCE (see appendix): Lodge's (1989) excellent *What Constitutes Good Sex Education?* and McLaughlin's (1989) *Sex Education*. Excellent work has been done too in the field of careers, trying to respond to the late twentieth-century challenge to young people's entry into the labour market and the adult world. Watts *et al*. (1981) survey the field in a most scholarly way, identifying the several theories that have driven the practice of careers guidance and counselling, from early talent-matching models (still influential in computerized matching programmes like JIIG-CAL), through the developmentalist approaches that saw job choice as the search to 'implement one's self concept', on to the realistic pessimism of the 'opportunity structuralists', who saw high unemployment as the clear indicator that choice and self-enhancement were no longer, if they ever had been, factors in job search – we simply took what was available – to a much more politicized 'community interaction' approach, in which clients would be helped to access the levers of power instead of engaging in an isolated, solitary search. All the theories have implications for the school counsellor or teacher working in this area and on the construction of curricular material (National Institute of Careers Education and Counselling, see appendix), but our focus remains that of the interactive nature of the counselling encounter. Whatever the transition facing the pupil-client, whatever the theories that underpin our perception of the change being negotiated, our response as counsellors will be successful or not according to how infused by the core conditions our encounter is.

CHILDREN IN TROUBLE

As teachers we regularly meet children who are 'in trouble': the pregnant (Bolton, 1980; Chandler, 1980), the bullied (Besag, 1989), the substance abuser (O'Connor, 1986), the anorexic (Slade and Duker, 1988), the stressed child (Robson, 1996). The list is, as Carey (1993) suggested, endless. Again, there are specialist texts on each of these topics; our task is to try to see some unifying characteristics that will help the counselling relationship. Chandler's analysis of the education of adolescent girls considers the issue of teenage pregnancy and identifies one such characteristic, which has a sound base in psychological theory: 'girls who take risks and become pregnant are not suffering as a rule from lack of instruction about contraception, they are suffering from lack of love'. It would be possible to generalize the quotation to include girls and boys in any kind of trouble.

It is an uncomfortable word, love, in a professional context. I once invited a tough head of a disruptive pupils unit, a former British Army unarmed combat instructor, to speak to trainee teachers about disruptive pupils. At the end of his interesting talk, I asked the group whether they would like to ask questions. Silence. So, to get things going, I said, 'Is there any particular theory that underlies the work you do in your unit?' I got a sergeant-major like stare, then, 'That's a real lecturer question, if I may say. I don't know any theories; I just love my kids.' It was a very powerful moment, and although the head, now sadly dead, 'did not know any theory', in my university lecturer way I was reminded of the great debate between Freud and the disciple he rejected, Sandor Ferenci. Ferenci's assertion that 'therapeutic movement occurs in direct proportion to the amount of love there is in the therapeutic relationship' was too unscientific for a man of Freud's medical training and background. I liked the link across the years and the professions between the bluff ex-soldier head and the Hungarian psychotherapist.

It is a link that Rogers (1951, 1983) makes explicit for teachers. In the earlier text, he presents with approval a 'clinical hypothesis' as he explores what makes counselling work. The second book applies his theory of counselling to the classroom: 'the term love, easily misunderstood though it may be, is the most useful term to describe a basic ingredient of the therapeutic relationship . . . therapeutic intervention at this emotional level, rather than interaction at a cognitive level, regardless of the context concerned, *is the effective ingredient for therapeutic growth*' (p. 160).

I suppose that is a fitting note on which to end. It puts the 'core conditions' for effective counselling into a nutshell: my clients will grow, develop to the extent to which they experience the counselling relationship as loving; my pupils will learn in the same climate. If either experience for them is not a loving one, then the positive change will be vitiated.

The position suggested above, the loving professional, is incredibly demanding, at a time when the demands on the profession are constant and many. How to stay whole under that stress is the focus of the final chapter.

Exercises

Chapter 8 argued that the specialness of issues which trouble pupils lies not so much in the content or material of the issue, but in ourselves as counsellors. What triggers in me can be pulled by someone else's pain, what deep waters in me can be stirred by an adolescent's grief, sexuality, lack of sense of self, feelings of being unloved? The following exercise needs to be done in a safe and nurturing group. It accepts Brammer and Shostrum's dictum that one of the tasks of counselling is to bring to the level of awareness material that is affecting my performance, but at a subconscious level. It also seeks to allow us to stand close to our own pain as a prerequisite to standing close to the pain of others.

Still waters

Take five minutes to jot down a list on the theme 'what bits of me might reduce my effectiveness as a counsellor with a pupil who has recently had a mother die?' Don't censor, let the ideas flow. Working with a partner, share your material to the extent it feels comfortable. Take it in turns to be counsellor and client. After both have had a turn, discuss the learning that has come from the exercise, and how it might influence your work with children.

It is useful over time to change the theme of the list:

- *a pregnant pupil;*
- *a substance abuser;*
- *a bully;*
- *a victim;*
- *a sexually abused pupil;*
- *a pupil who has just changed schools.*

The list is yours.

The following exercise permits an exploration of 'my experience of change'.

We have all experienced change in our lives. Some of it is eagerly sought-after (marriage), some is sad, perhaps reluctant (divorce); yet other change seems to come from nowhere, overwhelming us with its suddenness and its power (illness, death of loved ones). Draw to mind some significant change in your life and share the experience of it, in a way that feels safe and appropriate, with a partner. Bear in mind the Adams model of transition in the chapter. Your partner's task is to listen, reflect, help the exploration, make it safe for you to explore When you have finished (set a time limit of say ten minutes), change roles with your partner, and repeat the exercise for his or her benefit.

Finally, the whole group is asked to take part in a round (saying 'pass' is entirely acceptable), completing the phrase 'One thing I have learned about my own response to change is . . .' The group can close with a discussion of the implications for helping pupils to cope with change.

As always, exercises must be done in a supportive environment, and particularly when deep material is being touched upon, a trained leader should check that all participants are OK at the end of the session.

CHAPTER 10

Maintenance and growth for the teacher as counsellor

We constantly hear chief executives, personnel executives, government administrators, hospital administrators, headmasters [*sic*], and others in authority roles extolling the fact that the most important resource they have is people. Yet when it comes right down to it, how often do organisations protect, support and nurture this most valuable asset, the human resource?

(Sutherland and Cooper, 1990: p. 253)

Finally, this most valuable asset, ourselves. Every part of the previous chapters focuses on the well-being of our pupils, and a parallel respect for ourselves seems to demand that the same attention to our own well-being is a healthy and professional focus. Wounded carers work with diminished effect. Teaching and counselling are both enormously taxing, even when considered as discrete activities; counselling in a school environment, alongside all of the other multifarious tasks now given to teachers, makes very special demands on the practitioner, demands which are recognized and discussed by several authors in the June 1992 edition of the journal *Pastoral Care in Education*. An excellent symposium contributed to by Brockie, Lodge, McLaughlin, Best, Chappell, Hotham, Linge, Steadman, Sweetingham, Webb, Halfacree and Grant puts on to a front burner the almost culpable neglect by employers and senior managers of the well-being of teachers. I remember reading a judgment made in the High Court in 1994 that awarded £175,000 to a social worker, the compensation to be paid by his employer, Northumberland County Council, on the grounds that it had been responsible for two nervous breakdowns caused by his being given 'impossible workloads'. My thoughts on reading the case went to my own profession, at that time wrestling with the impossible workloads of SATs, league tables, OFSTED visitations, voluminous paperwork – oh, yes, and teaching the children. The 'John Walker' case seems important to me because it reminded employers that the mental well-being of employees should be considered part of the responsibility of the Health and Safety at Work legislation. While the case was in court, the Health and Safety Executive produced a document in which the following comments are made:

Mental health is a component of personal health, not a separate entity . . . the workplace [school] can be a stimulating and supportive environment and have a positive effect on mental health, but adverse situations can have a negative effect. There is thus great value in employers [governors] instituting an effective occupational health policy which routinely considers mental health aspects.

(HSE, 1993a)

There is no doubt that employers are liable if their work demands make staff physically *or mentally* ill, and detailed recommendations are made to employers about the ways in which they can try to meet their responsibilities. It is astonishing, given the High Court's decision in the John Walker case, that the Conservative government was in 1997 resisting the attempt by the European Parliament to protect worker health by establishing maximum working hours per week, on the grounds that numbers of working hours are not a health issue. Our professional associations ought to be noting and disseminating both the law and best practice on this issue – it is an important way of pre-empting stress in schools.

Consider the following comment: 'It is now generally admitted that they took too crudely a mechanistic view of their problems, stressed the factor of output too exclusively and thus antagonised many of the workers, who looked upon the new methods as merely devices of their employers to get more work done at less cost to themselves.' We could be forgiven for thinking that it had a modern ring to it. In fact, it is a critique by Flugel (cited by Brown, 1954) of the work of the early time and motion specialists who operated in the American steel industry fifty or more years ago. It is reassuring that one of the perpetrators of this experiment at the Bethlehem Steel works reflected later, 'It is a horrid life for any man to live, not being able to look any worker in the face without seeing hostility there, and a feeling that every man around you is an enemy.' Those crude early experiments in 'efficiency gains' have long since been discarded as doing no more than destroy the morale of the workforce, ultimately reducing quality. If we fail to address the stress levels, the mental health issues, in our own work a similar result can be expected. And stressed we are: a 1990 survey by the Centre for Organizational Health at Nottingham University (Cox, 1990) revealed that one in three teachers had stress levels high enough to warrant concern, one in four teachers said they would like to leave teaching altogether and an amazing three out of four wanted to change schools. Such levels of unhappiness should set managerial and employer alarm bells ringing; it is time to pay more than lip service to this 'most valuable asset, the human resource'.

We merit such care not only because of the Health and Safety Executive figures that 30 to 40 per cent of all sickness absence from work is the result of some mental or emotional disturbance (the HSE comment is that health care in this area 'should prove cost effective as health and productivity are closely linked'), not only because the children merit fit teachers and counsellors, but because long-term stress has a devastating effect on our general health. The relating of stress to heart disease, ulcers, allergies, asthma, eczema, migraine, hypertension and cerebrovascular disease has a strong scientific base (Sutherland and Cooper, 1990), and Temoshock and Heller (1984) have identified a stressed personality type (suppressed emotional responses, particularly anger, conformity, compliance and unassertiveness) which is more prone to all forms of cancer. This matches work done by Eysenck that suggested that personality tests were six times more accurate in predicting who would get heart disease or cancer than any of the customary physical clinical correlates (smoking, cholesterol level, alcohol consumption, etc.). We owe stress management to ourselves and our families.

People cope with stress in different ways. The ghoulish joke in my family is that when I am stressed I get a few weeks off by having a car crash! Having been almost killed on three occasions, I am taking the advice I am ladling out in this chapter. Of course, I did not decide to have a car crash (the first hot engine in my lap would have put me off the technique on subsequent occasions), but I have no doubt that my level of stress, trying to keep all the plates spinning, be here, there and everywhere, contributed to my accidents. But at the same time, I recall family members telling me to 'learn to say no', 'slow down' – all the things I had said to colleagues over the years. Stress creeps up on us; it occurs when the demands made of us exceed the resources we have to meet those demands, and is often accompanied by our having no control over the amount of material that is pouring in on us.

THE SCHOOL

If we are to reduce stress then the initial area of investigation has to be the employing organization. A paper by Cooper and Cartwright (1994) offers a summary of work done by Elkin and Rosch which examines possible organizational changes that can reduce stress. The detail of the work is not specific to schools, but the authors do identify that the trend of the strategies is to alter the culture of the workplace, particularly in involving employees at all levels of decision-making. This requires great managerial skill if disruption and time-wasting is not to be the result. Being even more general, we can use the 'dual-axis organizational analysis' (Figure 10.1) to allow us to check on areas of organizational weakness. We can consider that any organization, e.g. my school, can be run through a filter that looks at the following:

1. What is the challenge offered by this school? Specifics, at each operational level, whole-school issues, school–community issues, pastoral issues, academic issues, classroom performance issues, administrative issues, one-to-one counselling issues and so on. Then,
2. what are the levels of support that are given to members of the organization as they respond to the challenges? The members can list what factors make them feel supported, valued or nurtured in the school; and contraindications can be listed too. Then, an overview/profile (Figure 10.1) of the organizational climate can be gained. It may be a useful source of data for the governing body as they produce their 'occupational health policy'.

The protocol described above can be an invaluable diagnostic tool, and as a first step it yields significant insights into the organization. Clearly the key step is to enhance the 'support' dimensions of the organization, in order to develop maximum capacity to respond to challenge. From a management point of view, the government's running of the education service has been an unmitigated

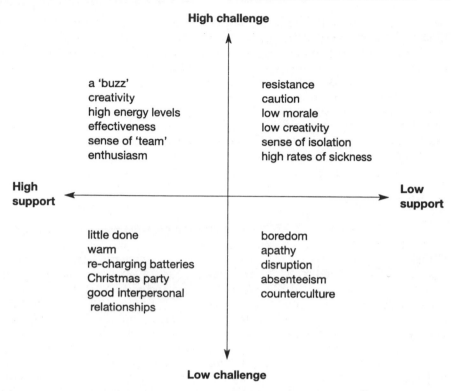

Figure 10.1 Dual-axis analysis of organizational climate

disaster, not because of some political or even educational disagreement that I may have with it, but because it has totally neglected the 'support' dimensions of its managerial responsibility. It is locked in a view of the teaching workforce that Brown castigated in his 1954 text — it sees us as motivated by greed and laziness, and tries to manage us by manipulating rewards and fear. As Brown says, the reality is that we are moved to truly great endeavours by other, more eccentric motives: pride, generosity, a desire for competence, a delight in achievement, a love of work and our pupils. To destroy that requires incompetence of great proportions, which relegates the 'invaluable asset, the human resource' to the status of workhorse.

We must, then, demand as a profession:

- the careful auditing of the occupational health policy in the school, and its implementation;
- the skill from our managers to be 'psycho-social leaders' (McGuiness, 1993c): that is, an ability, beyond task competence and financial competence, in addition to curricular planning skills, to communicate to staff that in confronting the challenges of this school, I will be concerned about your sense of safety; I will have a developmental view of your work; I will maintain respect for all colleagues as we respond to the climate of change in which we work; you will not be dehumanized, humiliated, bullied or abused; I will seek opportunities to promote your personal and professional development.

It sounds a bit idealistic, no doubt, but it is already a theme in the training of thousands of managers in the UK and USA, and, somewhat to the surprise of operational managers, is meeting bottom-line concerns. A clear organizational commitment to the health of the teaching staff is not only good for the school and its pupils, but also good for the teachers.

However, despite all the best efforts of high-quality organizations, employees will still face stress, and a consideration of how that stress can be managed at an individual level is appropriate. What happens when I am stressed, and how can I minimize the deleterious effect it has on my health and relationships with those around me?

BIOLOGY

Gregson and Looker (1994) offer a detailed account of what happens to our bodies when we are stressed. They argue that knowing what happens to us physically is a sound base for devising strategies for responding to the harmful consequences of raised stress levels. Three 'stress chemicals' in our body run the response to stress: adrenaline, noradrenaline and cortisol. It is their task to bring about appropriate bodily responses to the perceived or real threat, by altering the activity of various organs in the body. From an evolutionary point of view, our response to stress has advantaged us in coping with the demands of a primitive environment – OFSTED inspectors as a pack of wolves is perhaps an apt analogy! In the stressful situation of suddenly coming upon a pack of wolves, a sabre-toothed tiger or a mammoth, our ancestors had the option of 'fight' or 'flight' – not unlike ourselves. The physiological reaction to this perception has us releasing various amounts of the stress chemicals mentioned above. Thus anger (fight) provokes highly increased levels of noradrenaline and increased levels of adrenaline. Fear (flight) increases levels of both adrenaline and noradrenaline, but cortisol comes into play too; cortisol is the particular influence of depressive, submissive responses, rolling over helplessly, to hand over control totally to others. From our point of view, it is significant to note that levels of all three *decrease* when we are relaxed, meditating, being loved, loving, feeling supported and in harmony with the environment.

So, if we want to reduce the activity of the stress chemicals, some commitment to physical relaxation is important. Of course, the responses described are beneficial in meeting certain environmental conditions: the physiological changes are adaptive, in the sense that they produce the kind of changes in our body that will enhance survival chances if a wolf buries its fangs in our shoulder. Adrenaline and noradrenaline put the body into a state of high alert: fighting or escaping needs lots of oxygen, so breathing becomes deeper and rapid; in stress, we can feel constantly 'puffed'. To anticipate and facilitate high levels of activity the heart rate is increased and the force of the beat is upped, making the heart muscle work harder – constant stress leaves us with a heart labouring under the permanent impression that it is being chased by wolves! Just in case we are bitten, injured or wounded in some way, blood is altered so that it clots more easily and quickly – very adaptive for the primitive man lying with a hole in his shoulder and possibly bleeding to death, but not too grand for an overweight, middle-aged teacher whose heart is already working overtime to flee the potential attack of the wolves. Cortisol, the depressive, 'roll-over' chemical, mobilizes our glucose and fat stores, sensitizes the immune system and reduces inflammatory reactions. It is probably the chemical involved in the findings of Temoshock and Heller on increased proneness to cancer mentioned above.

We will have experienced a phenomenon, known as the Yerkes and Dodson–effect (see Yerkes and Dodson, 1993), that some levels of stress are actually enjoyable – that the physiological changes give us a high and are deliberately sought. What Yerkes and Dodson also tell us is that there is an (individual) optimum amount of stress and that once that peak is passed the negative effects begin to kick in. Thus we need to be alert for the danger signals and *to take action*. Which of the following symptoms have you experienced in the past year: awareness of the heartbeat, palpitations; awareness of rapid, shallow breathing, huge sighs; dry mouth, heartburn, queasy stomach, diarrhoea, constipation; muscular tension in the jaws, neck and shoulders, aches, pains, cramps; hyperactivity, finger-drumming, foot-tapping, nail-biting, trembling hands; fatigue, exhaustion, disturbed sleep patterns, feeling faint or dizzy, sweats, frequent desire to urinate, changes in levels of smoking (up), alcohol intake (up) or sexual activity (down)? All of them? Join the club. We are living highly stressed lives, and while the symptoms above can be the result of other life factors, they are identified by Gregson and Looker (1994) as indicators of stress.

Since we have begun with the physiological, the initial responses will be physiological. Given that the organizational climate has done all it can to enhance the working conditions of the teacher (and this needs to be a very serious first step), the individual can begin to look at the potential of physiological responses. Cooper and Sutherland describe a 'type A personality', who is at high risk as a potential heart attack victim. Such a person 'needs' to be always in control, consistently wants to achieve more and more to tighter deadlines, sees opposition and idleness in others as thwarting his or her work, is often impatient and aggressive over minor issues. The levels of adrenaline and noradrenaline to sustain this highly stressed lifestyle are so high as to trigger the physiological responses outlined above. During bouts of anger, for example, research suggests that high levels of noradrenaline can produce plaque rupture, coronary thrombosis, coronary spasm and the initiation of fatal arrhythmic heart behaviour.

The major approach patterns to control of the negative elements of stress are as follows:

- Learning to relax (relaxation exercises, yoga, meditation, guided imagery). An excellent text for this is Oaklander's book, written with pupils in mind, but full of helpful techniques for all of us. Published in 1978, it uses gestalt techniques to develop tranquillity and serenity. Typically, the response of type A people is to say, 'I can't relax.' The reality is that they are choosing not to relax; relaxation, like every other skill, can be learned.
- Breathing exercises. Kilty and Bond (1991) have produced an excellent manual in which they offer help for ameliorating breathing techniques. Fried (1993) offers a more theoretical analysis of both the psychological and the physiological aspects of breathing.

- Taking exercise. Walking, swimming, gardening all involve us in the kind of physiological activity that has the body use the physiological changes in a way that 'sitting and fuming' – or even thinking – cannot.
- Caffeine stimulates the production of both adrenaline and noradrenaline. To take it on top of stress can intensify the negative physiological consequences described earlier.

INTRAPERSONAL

Having looked at the organization and the body as areas for attention in reducing stress, it would be strange if, in a book on counselling, we did not pay attention to the 'in me' dimension. Another source of stress is the energy expended in the suppression, denial or tight control of powerful emotional material. A requirement of the BAC on counsellors is that they have regular supervision, i.e. that for about one hour for every six hours of counselling, the counsellor should explore with a superviser any key issues that are around – usually technical (am I doing it right?), ethical (what kind of confidentiality can I really offer a minor in school?) or personal (this client has awakened 'x' powerful feeling in me). The benefits of some peer support groups for teachers are evident, but to be realistic, and given the time boundaries they work under, that is probably some time away. We need to be aware that counselling is not just for our pupils, and to use counselling as a response to stress when we feel it appropriate. Over half of the GP surgeries in the UK now offer a counselling service – ask for it if you would like to use it. At the very least, find a trusted friend and unload from time to time. You can do it on a reciprocal basis: peer co-counselling.

INTERPERSONAL RESPONSES

Perhaps Sartre was right, and hell is really 'other people'. It is certainly the case that stress is frequently other people. They create difficulties for us, make inappropriate demands on us, let us down, fail to support us, and the consequent stress is often difficult to dissipate. My own experience is that a key element in controlling interpersonal stress is learning how to say 'no'. It takes us back to the action phase of counselling and the role-play/modelling approach to things we find it difficult to do. The exercises at the end of this chapter will offer some suggestions here.

Being ourselves is another important way of coping with interpersonal stress: assertiveness, not aggression and its I win–you lose ethic, not submissiveness and its you win–I lose ethic, but assertiveness, which permits a win–win possibility via negotiation and conflict resolution. The Kilty and Bond (1991) text already mentioned is excellent on assertiveness development.

I have said nothing about the cognitive, time management approaches to stress management, not because I do not think they help, but because they give a different slant to stress: I am stressed because in some sense I am inefficient. That may well be the case, and the cognitive approach does help us to be more efficient. Nevertheless, most stress seems to come from the need we have to respond to demands beyond the contractual and deeper than the cognitive.

No teacher or counsellor should feel lonely as a professional – being part of a team allows stress to be dissipated. Working in company with others is reassuring – that is the presumption of the exercises at the end of this chapter.

Exercises

Looking after ourselves is probably one of the least developed capacities – workers in the caring professions are notoriously cavalier about their own health. So much is that the case that it is important to stress the ethical demand on us to stay as healthy as we can for the good of our clients and pupils. The audit that follows tries to help in that ethical response.

Swimming against the tide

With a partner, make a list of the stressors that currently send adrenaline, noradrenaline and cortisol coursing through your body in excessive amounts. Categorize them as

- *organizational;*
- *physical;*
- *intrapersonal;*
- *interpersonal.*

Sometimes drawing a picture of them liberates our ability to face them. What is the organization visually, my shoulder, my head seen from the inside, my deputy principal? In a counselling encounter, take it in turns to explore the stress.

Action planning

Using the exercises in Chapter 7, look at the options open to you in this situation. Be creative: not 'I can't', only 'I am choosing not to'. Remember you are coping with factors that have the capacity to make you ill or even kill you. Look at the following:

- *How can I change the organization to be a more teacher-friendly place? Whom do I need to help? What actions do I need to take? (See Chapter 8 for strategies.)*
- *What is my body asking me to do? Relaxation, exercise, diet, stop smoking, massage, aromatherapy, tai-chi, yoga?*
- *Do I need counselling, peer support, a good friend to chat to? What do I have to do to supply that need?*
- *Who is bugging me? How can I respond in an assertive way, making appropriate demands in a non-aggressive way? Do I need to practise in role-play, or have someone model the behaviour for me as an exemplar?*

Learning from our pupils

Early in this book, at the beginning of Chapter 2, I shared a vision of the uniqueness of children that came from Pablo Casals. I find it a real challenge, since much of my work has been with the so-called disruptive pupil. It is sometimes hard to find the jewel of dignity in such pupils. I have seen crude racism in pupils, gross ill manners, exploitative sexuality, cruelty and even sadism. But I still feel comfortable with Oaklander's (1978) comment: 'Children are our finest teachers. They already know how to grow, how to develop, how to feel, laugh and cry and get mad, what is right for them and what is not right for them, what they need. They already know how to love and be joyful and to live life to the fullest, to work and to be strong and full of energy. All they (and the child within us) need is the space to do it' (p. 324).

The powerful 'empty chair' technique, frequently used by gestalt therapists, involves the client in identifying two 'selves' who are in conflict; for example, the 'I want to stop smoking' self and the 'I really enjoy smoking and don't want to quit' self. Each self is assigned a chair, the two chairs are placed facing each other about a yard apart, and the counsellor facilitates a dialogue between the two selves. 'Which self is most "you" at the moment?' 'The smoker.' 'OK. Then sit in the chair labelled "smoker John", and imagine that in the chair opposite you is "non-smoker John". What would you say to him? Just tell him how you feel right now.' When 'smoker John' has finished, the counsellor unobtrusively invites him to swap chairs. 'Change chairs. OK. You are now non-smoker John. You've heard smoker John's feelings on this. How do you react to what you have heard?' The dialogue is under way, with the counsellor gently maintaining the momentum – not interpreting or intervening, simply asking for the switch when it seems that one of the characters has ended his piece of dialogue.

The following exercise uses that technique, but instead of facilitating an internal discussion, it is used to generate a conversation with an outside person.

> Here are two chairs. I would like you to try to be as open and honest as you can. This chair is yours, the teacher's – opposite is the pupil's chair. Can you choose any pupil you currently work with, and make the other chair hers or his. Sit opposite the 'pupil'. Ask him or her, 'If you could wave a magic wand and make me a better teacher, what one thing would you change?' Actually say it to the empty chair, imagining the pupil to be there; then sit in the pupil's chair and answer the query, as if you were the pupil. If it feels appropriate, engage in a dialogue, changing chairs to remind you to keep in role. You may want to do the exercise using different pupils, who may need different things from you.

This is a very hard exercise, because it involves self-critical auditing, but it is a very professional exercise precisely because of that. It seems like a sound and challenging strategy for the last exercise of the book.

Epilogue

The governors of schools, senior managers and teaching staff in schools may be a little surprised that I have not pushed harder for the proliferation of the school counsellor. That I have not done this is not the result of a view that schools do not need counsellors – it is the consequence of my taking a different perspective. My argument is not about how precisely to organize the staffing of schools, it has been more straightforward: that the pupils and staff of our schools need ready and easy access to counselling expertise, just as such skills are increasingly the available norm in the world of work. The way of providing that access will vary from school to school.

Those who make decisions about how to staff schools, I hope, now have a greater insight into the complexity of counselling, its multi-level nature, the common skills it shares with good teaching and the, thankfully rare, occasions when the school's responsibility to the humans who inhabit it involves the provision of very specialist counselling services. The book has recounted the increasingly demanding way in which the High Court is interpreting the Health and Safety at Work legislation to include social and emotional health. Clearly, as education professionals we need to have strategic responses to these demands.

I close, nevertheless, not on legal requirements and fear of litigation, but on the ethical demand implied in the Pablo Casals quotation at the opening of Chapter 2. Being humans, having profound, intrinsic value, we merit the provision of services that meet all our developmental needs: the academic, social and emotional. Schools must offer counselling expertise to their staff and pupils. Not to do so is unethical.

Appendix: sources of further development

British Association for Counselling: 1 Regent Place, Rugby, Warwickshire CV21 2PJ. The Association offers information about counselling and counsellors, and provides support training and education, as well as accrediting individual practitioners. A Code of Ethics for school counsellors and teachers using counselling skills is available.

Centre for Stress Management, 156 Westcombe Hill, London SE3 7DH. Provides stress management courses and training for practitioners in the field.

Counselling Psychology Division of the British Psychological Society, St Andrews House, 48 Princess Road East, Leicester LE1 7DR. Has a similar set of aims to those of the BAC, but is based in the psychological paradigm. All chartered counsellors have to be graduate psychologists. An appropriate home for educational psychologists or teachers with psychology degrees.

Human Potential Resources Group, Dept of Educational Studies, University of Surrey, Guildford GU2 5XH. Prolific producers of training manuals (e.g. Kilty and Bond, 1991) across a wide range of humanistic approaches to counsellng.

The National Association for Pastoral Care in Education, Education Department, University of Warwick, Coventry CV4 7AL. This highly influential and professional association has the school as its major focus. While not focusing specifically on counselling, it offers a constant stream of highly pertinent cognate literature in its journal, frequently cited in this text.

The National Institute of Careers Education and Counselling is a research and curriculum development centre of international standing. Details of their work are available from Dr Bill Law, NICEC, Sheraton House, Castle Park, Cambridge CB3 0AX.

Both the BAC and the BPS produce practitioner journals, and the *British Journal of Guidance and Counselling* is published four times a year by Carfax, PO Box 25, Abingdon, Oxfordshire OX14 3UE.

Local colleges and universities offer training courses, from beginners' courses to advanced courses.

The Centre for Studies in Counselling at The School of Education, Leazes Road, Durham DH1 1TA, offers short courses in counselling, basic and advanced certificate courses, an advanced diploma and an MA in counselling. There is a full-time MA in guidance and counselling for students from outside the region; the other courses are offered on a part-time basis. The School has a strong research ethos, and a number of counsellors are completing doctoral programmes there.

National Foundation for Educational Research, Darville House, 2 Oxford Road East, Windsor SL4 1DF.

Bibliography

Adams, J. (1976) *Understanding and Managing Personal Change*. Oxford: Martin Robertson.

Adams, S. (1990) Child self-protection: concerns about classroom approaches. *Pastoral Care in Education*, **8**(3), 3–6.

American Psychiatric Association (1980) *Diagnostic and Statistical Manual of Mental Disorders*. Washington, DC: APA.

Argyle, M. (1988) *Bodily Communication*. London: Methuen.

Berne, E. (1961) *Transactional Analysis in Psychotherapy*. New York: Grove Press.

Berne, E. (1972) *What Do You Say After You Say Hello?* London: Corgi.

Besag, C. (1989) *Bullies and Victims in Schools: A Guide to Understanding and Management*. Milton Keynes: Open University Press.

Best, R.E., Jarvis, C. and Ribbins, P. (1977) Pastoral care: concept and process. *British Journal of Educational Studies*, **35**(2), 124–35.

Best, R.E., Jarvis, C., Ribbins, P. and Oddy, D. (1983) *Education and Care*. London: Heinemann.

Bishop, M. (1990) Adolescence and the need for counselling in schools. *Pastoral Care in Education*, **8**(2), 3–10.

Blocher, D. (1974) *Developmental Counselling*. New York: Ronald Press.

Bolton, F.G. (1980) *The Pregnant Adolescent*. London: Sage Library of Social Research.

Brammer, L.M. and Shostrum, E.L. (1968) *Therapeutic Psychology*, 2nd edn. Englewood Cliffs, NJ: Prentice Hall.

Brammer, L.M. and Shostrum, E.L. (1977) *Therapeutic Psychology*, 3rd edn. Englewood Cliffs, NJ: Prentice Hall.

Brammer, L.M. and Shostrum, E.L. (1982) *Therapeutic Psychology*, 4th edn. Englewood Cliffs, NJ: Prentice Hall.

Brammer, L.M., Shostrum, E.L. and Abrego, P. (1989) *Therapeutic Psychology: Fundamentals of Counseling and Psychotherapy*, 5th edn. Englewood Cliffs, NJ: Prentice Hall.

Brandes, D. (1981) *The Hope Street Experience*. Leeds: Access Publications.

British Association for Counselling (1992) *Code of Ethics and Practice for Counsellors*. Rugby: BAC.

British Psychological Society (1995) The recovery of memories in clinical practice. Working Party on Recovered Memories. *The Psychologist*, **8**(5), 209–14.

Brown, J.A.C. (1954) *The Social Psychology of Industry*. Harmondsworth: Penguin.

Bruner, J.S., Goodnow, J.S. and Austin, G.A. (1956) *A Study of Thinking*. New York: Wiley.

Burns, R.B. (1979) *The Self Concept: Theory, Measurement, Development and Behaviour*. Harlow: Longman.

Burns, R.B. (1982) *Self Concept Development and Education*. New York: Holt, Rinehart and Winston.

Cadbury Report (1988) *Building a Stronger Relationship between Business and Secondary Education*. London: Confederation of British Industry.

Carey, P. (1993) Dealing with pupils' life crises: a model for action. *Pastoral Care in Education*, **11**(3), 12–18.

Carkhuff, R.R. and Berenson, B.G. (1977) *Beyond Counselling and Therapy*, 2nd edn. New York: Holt, Rinehart and Winston.

Cartwright, D. and Zander, A. (1968) *Group Dynamics: Theory and Research*. London: Tavistock.

Casals, P. (1969) Conversation with Golda Meir, at the performance of his oratorio *El Pesebre* in Israel, British Broadcasting Corporation.

Chandler, E.M. (1980) *Educating Adolescent Girls*. London: Unwin Educational Books.

Coleman, J.C. (1980) *The Nature of Adolescence*. London: Methuen.

Cooper, C.L. and Cartwright, S. (1994) Stress management interventions in the workplace: stress counselling and stress audits. *British Journal of Guidance and Counselling*, **22**(1), 65–73.

Corey, G. (1986) *Theory and Practice of Counselling and Psychotherapy*, 3rd edn. Monterey, CA: Brookes/Cole.

Courtois, C. (1988) *Healing the Incest Wound*. New York: W.W. Norton and Company.

Cox, T. (1990) Survey for NUT on occupational stress, carried out by Centre for Organizational Health, Nottingham University.

Cronbach, L. (1970) *Essentials of Psychological Testing*. New York: Harper and Row.

Daws, P.D. (1967) What will the school counsellor do? *Educational Research*, **9**, 83–92.

Daws, P.D. (1976) *Early Days: A Personal Review of the Beginnings of Counselling in English Education, 1964–1974*. London: Careers Research Advisory Centre.

Dearing Report (1994) *Final Report on the National Curriculum and Its Assessment*. London: SCAA Publications.

de Bono, E. (1990) *I Am Right, You Are Wrong*. Harmondsworth: Penguin.

DES (1979) *Aspects of Secondary Education in England*. London: HMSO.

DES (1987) *Teaching as a Career*. London: HMSO.

Donaldson, M. (1982) *Children's Minds*. London: Fontana.

Egan, G. (1986) *The Skilled Helper*. Monterey, CA: Brookes/Cole.

Egan, G. (1993) *Adding Value: A Shared-Models Blueprint for Management*. Chicago: Loyola University.

Eiser, C., Havermans, T., Rolph, P. and Rolph, J. (1995) The place of bereavement and loss in the curriculum: teachers' attitudes. *Pastoral Care in Education*, **13**(4), 32–7.

Elliott, M. (1990) A response to Steve Adams. *Pastoral Care in Education*, **8**(3), 7–9.

Elton Report (1989) *Enquiry into Discipline in Schools*. London: HMSO.

Eysenck, H.J. (1953) *Uses and Abuses of Psychology*. Harmondsworth: Penguin.

Frankl, V. (1964) *Man's Search for Meaning*. New York: Simon and Schuster.

Fried, R. (1993) *The Psychology and Physiology of Breathing*. New York: Plenum Press.

Gelatt, H.B. (1962) Decision-making: a conceptual frame of reference for counselling. *Journal of Counselling Psychology*, **9**, 240–5.

Gelatt, H.B. (1989) Positive understanding: a new decision-making framework for counselling. *Journal of Counselling Psychology*, **35**, 252–6.

Gilliland, J. and McGuiness, J. (1989) Counselling and special educational needs. In N. Jones (ed.), *Special Educational Needs Review*, Vol. 2. Lewes: Falmer Press.

Gilmore, S. (1980) A comprehensive theory for eclectic intervention. *International Journal for the Advancement of Counselling*, **3**, 185–210.

Gordon, T. (1974) *Teacher Effectiveness Training*. New York: P.H. Wyden.

Gregson, O. and Looker, T. (1994) The biological basis of stress management. *British Journal of Guidance and Counselling*, **22**(1), 13–26.

Hamblin, D. (1974) *The Teacher and Counselling*. Oxford: Blackwell.

Hamblin, D. (1993) *The Teacher and Counselling*. New York: Simon and Schuster.

Harris, B. (1996) Pastoral provision and the GCSE. *Pastoral Care in Education*, **14**(3), 6–11.

Health and Safety Executive (1993a) *Mental Health at Work*. London: HSE, Employment Department Group.

Health and Safety Executive (1993b) *Mental Distress at Work*. London: HSE, Employment Department Group.

Heisler, V. (1961) Towards a process model of psychological health. *Journal of Counselling Psychology*, **11**(1), 59–62.

Heppner, P. (1989) Identifying the complexities within clients' thinking and decision-making. *Journal of Counselling Psychology*, **35**(2), 252–6.

Herman, J.L. (1992) *Trauma and Recovery: From Domestic Abuse to Political Terror*. London: Pandora, HarperCollins.

Herr, E. (1976) *Does Counselling Work?* The Hague: International Round Table for the Advancement of Counselling, Martinus Nijhoff.

Hufton, A. (1986) An investigation into loss, grief and bereavement, with special reference to adolescence. Unpublished MA study, Durham University Library.

Hutton, W. (1994a), Happiness that money truly cannot buy. *Guardian*, 27 December.

Hutton, W. (1994b) Money before machines. *Guardian*, 3 January.

Jahoda, M. (1982) *Employment and Unemployment: A Social-Psychological Analysis*. Cambridge: Cambridge University Press.

Kilty, J. and Bond, M. (1991) *Practical Methods of Dealing with Stress*. Guildford: Human Potential Resource Group, University of Surrey.

Kitchener, E. (1984) Intuition, critical evaluation and ethical principles: the foundations for ethical decisions in counselling psychology. *Counselling Psychologist*, **12**(3), 43–55.

Krumboltz, J. D. and Thoresen, C. E. (1969) *Counselling Methods*. New York: Holt, Rinehart and Winston.

Krumboltz, J. D. and Thoresen, C. E. (1976) *Behavioral Counselling: Cases and Technique*. New York: Holt, Rinehart and Winston.

Lang, P. (1988) *Thinking about PSE in the Primary School*. Oxford: Blackwell.

Lawlor, S. (1990) *Teachers Mistaught*. London: Centre for Policy Studies.

Lawrence, D. (1973) *Improved Reading through Counselling*. London: Ward Lock.

Leaman, O. (1995) *Death and Loss: Compassionate Approaches in the Classroom*. London: Cassell.

Lodge, C. (1989) *What Constitutes Good Sex Education?* London: National Association for Pastoral Care in Education, Issues Document, 'Sex Education'.

McGuiness, J. (1982) *Planned Pastoral Care*. London: McGraw-Hill.

McGuiness, J. (1983) Secondary education for all? In F.J. Coffield and R.D. Goodings (eds), *Sacred Cows in Education*. Edinburgh: Edinburgh University Press.

McGuiness, J. (1988) Let's start at the very beginning. In P. Lang (ed.), *Thinking about PSE in the Primary School*. Oxford: Blackwell.

McGuiness, J. (1989) *A Whole School Approach to Pastoral Care*. London: Kogan Page.

McGuiness, J. (1992) *El papel de 'Counselling' en la Gestion de Cambio*. Madrid: Hurst (Europe) Associates.

McGuiness, J. (1993a) *Teachers, Pupils and Behaviour: A Managerial Approach*. London: Cassell.

McGuiness, J. (1993b) The National Curriculum: the manufacture of pigs' ears out of best silk. *British Journal of Guidance and Counselling*, **21**(1), 106–11.

McGuiness, J. (1993c) Managing nicely: the role of counselling in the management of change. Paper presented at International Conference, Counselling in the Workplace, University of Durham.

McLaughlin, C. (1989) *Sex Education*. London: National Association for Pastoral Care in Education, Issues Document.

McLaughlin, C., Clark, P. and Chisolm, M. (1996) *Counselling and Guidance in Schools: Developing Policy and Practice*. London: David Fulton.

Maher, P. (1987) *Child Abuse: The Educational Perspective*. Oxford: Blackwell.

Maher, P. (1990) Child protection: another view. *Pastoral Care in Education*, **8**(3), 9–12.

Manpower Services Commission (1982) *Youth Task Group Report*. London: MSC.

May, R. (1969) *Existential Psychology*. New York: Random House.

Mead, G.H. (1934) *Mind, Self and Society from the Standpoint of a Social Behaviourist*. Chicago: University of Chicago Press.

Moore, D., Decker, S., Greenwood, A. and Kirby, S. (1996) Research into demand for counselling/therapeutic provision in a group of secondary schools. *Pastoral Care in Education*, **14**(1), 3–6.

Morrell, F. (1989) *Children of the Future*. London: The Hogarth Press.

Murgatroyd, S. and Woolf, R. (1982) *Coping with Crisis*. London: Harper and Row.

Nelson-Jones, R. (1982) *The Theory and Practice of Counselling Psychology*. New York: Holt Psychology.

NFER (1980) *Lewis Counselling Inventory*. Windsor: NFER.

Norcross, J.C. and Grencavage, L. (1989) Eclecticism and integration in counselling and psychotherapy: major themes and obstacles. *British Journal of Guidance and Counselling*, **17**(3), 227–43.

Norcross, J.C. and Guy, J.D. (1989) Ten therapists: the process of being and becoming. In W. Dryden and L. Spurling (eds), *On Becoming a Psychotherapist*. London: Routledge.

Oaklander, V. (1978) *Windows on Our Children: A Gestalt Therapy Approach to Children and Adolescents*. Moab, UT: Real People Press.

O'Connor, D. (1986) Glue sniffing and solvent abuse. Cheadle Boys' and Girls' Welfare Society, available from University of Durham Library.

El País (1995) The case of 'Leonardino', a sexually abused child. *El País*, 25 March.

Perls, F. (1973) *Gestalt Approach and Eyewitness to Therapy*. New York: Bantam.

Piaget, J. (1926) *The Language and Thought of the Child*. London: Routledge and Kegan Paul.

Piaget, J. (1952) *The Origins of Intelligence in the Child*. New York: International Universities Press.

Piaget, J. and Inhelder, B. (1958) *The Growth of Logical Awareness from Childhood to Adolescence*. London: Routledge and Kegan Paul.

Robson, M. (1993) Stress in adolescence. *Counselling Psychology Quarterly*, **6**(3), 217–28.

Robson, M. (1996) Stress and children. Unpublished PhD thesis, University of Durham.

Rogers, C. (1942) *Counselling and Psychotherapy*. Boston: Houghton Mifflin.

Rogers, C. (1951) *Client Centered Therapy*. London: Constable.

Rogers, C. (1983) *Freedom to Learn for the Eighties*. Columbus, OH: Merrill Publishing Company.

Rokeach, M. (1968) Beliefs, attitudes and values: a theory of organisation and change. Offprint, available from University of Durham Library.

Simon, S.B. (1978) *Values Clarification: A Handbook of Practical Strategies*. New York: Hart.

Slade, R. and Duker, M. (1988) *Anorexia Nervosa and Bulimia*. Milton Keynes: Open University Press.

Snygg, A.W. and Combs, D. (1959) *Individual Behaviour*. New York: Harper and Row.

Soyinka, W. (1972) *Man Died: Prison Notes*. London: Collins.

Stott, D.H. (1976) *Bristol Social Adjustment Guide*. London: Hodder and Stoughton.

Strupp, R. (1986) Psychotherapy: research, practice and public policy. *American Psychologist*, **4**, 120–30.

Sutherland, V.J. and Cooper, C. (1990) *Understanding Stress: A Psychological Perspective for Health Professionals*. London: Chapman and Hall.

Temoshock, L. and Heller, B.W. (1984) On comparing apples, oranges and fruit salad: a methodological overview of medical outcome studies in psychosocial oncology. In *Psychosocial Stress and Cancer*. Chichester: John Wiley.

Times Educational Supplement (1994) School counsellors. 7 October.

Truax, C.B. and Carkhuff, R.R. (1967) *Towards Effective Counselling and Psychotherapy*. Chicago: Aldine Publishing.

Tudor, K. and Worrall, M. (1994) Congruence re-considered. *British Journal of Guidance and Counselling*, **22**(2), 197–207.

Vigotsky, L.S. (1964) *Thought and Language*. Cambridge, MA: MIT Press.

Wall, W.D. (1968) *Adolescents in School and Society*. Slough: NFER.

Ward, B. and associates (1988/9) *Good Grief: Talking and Learning about Loss and Death*, two volumes. London: Jennifer Kingsley.

Watts, A.G., Super, D.E. and Kidd, J.M. (1981) *Career Development in Britain*. Cambridge: Hobson Press.

Wells, R. (1988) *Helping Children Cope with Grief*. London: Sheldon Press.

Index

Yerkes, R.M. and Dodson, J.D. (1993) The relation of strength of stimulus to rapidity of habit-formation. *J. Comp. Neurol. Psychol.*, **18**, 459–82 (1908), discussed in D. Childs (ed.), *Psychology and the Teacher*. London: Cassell, pp. 58–60.

Yule, W. and Gold, A. (1993) *Wise before the Event: Coping with Crises in Schools*. London: Calouste Gulbenkian Foundation.